The Peacemakers

Restoring Love in the World through Stories of Compassion and Wisdom

Compiled by Shanda Trofe
Foreword by Louise Huey Greenleaf

THE PEACEMAKERS

Restoring Love in the World through Stories of Compassion and Wisdom

Transcendent Publishing
P.O. Box 66202
St. Pete Beach, FL 33736
(800) 232-5087
www.TranscendentPublishing.com

ISBN-10: 0-9982869-3-1

ISBN-13: 978-0-9982869-3-8

Library of Congress Control Number: 2016918716

Compiled by Shanda Trofe

Edited by Kathleen Marusak

Cover Design by Pixel Studio

Printed in the United States of America.

PRAISE FOR THE PEACEMAKERS

“Twenty one unique and remarkable, highly-relatable, every-day women share their personal recipes, prayers, step-by-step guidelines, heartfelt stories and affirmations for unity and conciliation in *The Peacemakers*, a powerful new book by Transcendent Publishing. What the world needs now — more than ever, is precisely this sort of encouragement for ordinary and extraordinary people alike to embrace simple practices of self-compassion and love for others.

“Peace starts within. We learn in these highly approachable pages that person-by-person, heart-centered living creates a ripple that builds a wave of kindness to uplift others and unify our communities. From an Angel Card Reader to Kindness Warrior, non-profit leader to Shamanic practitioner—entrepreneur to Interspecies Communicator, women from all walks of life awaken the spirit within us that is yearning to give peace a chance. Take a first step from these motivational voices by starting with some small illumination each and every day.

“Look at this as a guidebook to restore hope within you and inspire you to shine your goodness in the world around you.”

~**Frances Rivetti,** British/American independent journalist, author of *Fog Valley Crush* and *Fog Valley Winter*
www.southernsonomacountrylife.com

"This book couldn't come at a better time in our history. A time when sadness and anger flow from the media, when negativity clutters up our news feeds, the authors of this compilation have come together to do their part to spread love and light to our planet. Blessed are the peacemakers, and blessed are all who have the pleasure of reading this compilation."

~ **Sunny Dawn Johnston,** best-selling author of *Invoking the Archangels* and *The Love Never Ends,*
www.sunnydawnjohnston.com

"*The Peacemakers* is a soothing collection of soulful essays that reminds us of an essential truth—that peace starts from within. By sharing their thoughtful reflections on life's lessons and practical tools for a pathway to a love-led life, these wise women invite us to open our hearts and minds to a new way of being. Truth and comfort lie within these pages."

~**Christine Sheehy,** Messaging Coach & Author
www.christinesheehy.co

"Many reports have shown that survivors of childhood abuse often endure lifelong symptoms such as depression, anxiety, eating disorders, and various self-harming behavior. Faith Klingsporn is a survivor of severe abuse for many of her childhood years. Even when she did ask for help as a child, she was told to not talk about it.

"I started working with Faith in 2006 when she began coming to me for therapy to treat symptoms of post-traumatic stress. I was immediately impressed by her courage and determination to understand and heal from the trauma she carried within her.

"Therapy is not an easy path to choose for most people. Faith said many times that the hard work and frustration she was experiencing was worth it in order to heal. She compared it to an exciting spiritual journey filled with meaning and purpose.

"It has been an honor to work with Faith."

~**Dan G Connor,** Licensed Psychotherapist

At the deepest level of creation, all beings are seeking peace. Underneath the outer shell of every human being beats a heart created in pure love. I pray from this consciousness, visualizing each person connecting with their divine selves and acting from that sacred place.

I envision the world enveloped in peace and wrapped in a warm, flowing channel of divine love. In gratitude, I affirm: Divine love is flowing, connecting, and healing the world and everyone in it.

I, too, act upon my inner divinity, recognizing that every word I speak and action I take can be done in peaceful, loving, and faith-filled ways. Divine love flows from my heart to bless the world.

~ *Author Unknown*

CONTENTS

FOREWORD
by Louise Huey Greenleaf

Peace. Just the word itself, whether spoken, read, or experienced, immediately ushers in an emotional sense of tranquil equanimity. Perhaps it comes through simple acts of kindness toward another—such as offering a prayer, a smile, or a warm embrace. It is felt in the calming, quiet places in nature or through meditation, where we can seize countless opportunities to center our thoughts as we still the souls of others, as well as our own. For it is without question, that no matter what trials, snares, conflicts or joys we encounter, whether good or bad, happy or sad, peace may surely be procured through the countless tiny miracles God and the universe provide for *all* of us, *every single moment* of *every single day*—if we choose to receive them. It is without question that peace is a state of mind that quiets and relieves what is our deepest and truest essence.

In this exquisitely written multi-author collective, you will be inspired by personal accounts composed by each of the talented writers whose works fill its pages. They are an eclectic group of Peacemakers whose words are sure to move your emotions as you ingest their riveting stories and poems. They transport their readers, yes, you and me, to the realization that to hold the title "Peacemaker," is *not* just limited to well-known wise philosophers, ancient masters or world diplomats. We *all* possess the ability to be depicted as *Peacemakers,* whether through a mother's love and hope for her child's future, a widow's desire to carry on her husband's legacy of kindness, or realizing the importance of practicing self-love for the good of our physical as well as psychological well-being. Each and every chapter will surely cause your heart and mind to be pervaded with peace.

The peacemakers is the newest multi-author book published by Shanda Trofe, who founded Spiritual Writers Network in 2012, and is President & CEO of Transcendent Publishing. She is the Bestselling author of *Write from the Heart*, and *Authorpreneur: How to Build an Empire and Become the AUTHOR-ity in Your Business.* She is an author coach and mentor to hundreds of aspiring writers who strive to share their gift of the written word. Through her quarterly contests and book writing courses, she has fulfilled the dreams of so many to become published authors—including myself. Through her expert knowledge, wisdom, and loving spirit, she embraces each one of her clients and students with open arms, and encourages ALL to reach their full potential as a writer. Shanda is a very special lady, and a beautiful gift to the world. She is an angel of love, and a true *Peacemaker.*

Louise Huey Greenleaf is an award-winning author and poet. Her works are included in five multi-author books with Spiritual Writers Network and Transcendent Publishing; *Touched by an Angel: A Collection of Divinely Inspired Stories and Poems*/ Titanium Angel; *Whispers of the Soul: A Poetry Anthology* (3rd Place Quarterly Contest Winner)/SUCCUMP-TION-ACITY; *The Best of Spiritual Writers Network 2014*/A Precious Memory; *Illuminations of the Soul: A Poetry Anthology*/Millions of Reasons to Smile Today; *Finding Our Wings: An Angelic Collection of Stories and Poems*/Angels Watching Over Me (Title by Krista Gawronski and Louise Huey Greenleaf), *The Invisible Thread: Real Stories of Synchronicity with Sunny Dawn Johnston and Friends*/Silky Tales of Eternal Grace, Published by OptiMystic Press.

INTRODUCTION

"Peace can become a lens through which you see the world. Be it. Live it. Radiate it out. Peace is an inside job."
~WAYNE DYER

I'd like to take a moment of your time, if you will, before you delve into the pages ahead, to ask you to reflect on one word: Peace. I ask you to step away from the busyness around you, and truly think about what the word *peace* means to you. Is it just a word you brush off? Or is there something more, something deeper that the very thought of peace conjures up within you? And more importantly, what actions do you take each day to create peace in our world? Are you doing your part? Or do you think of this task as a lost cause?

Perhaps you have come to accept the world as it is. You may be wondering, what can one do to create peace in the world at a time like this? In a world that seems to have lost its way, when hope is shattered and tales of hate and sadness clutter up our newsfeeds? What can one person possibly do to create change when everything appears to be so far gone?

That's one way to look at it. But the authors of this collection have encouraged me to look at peace from a new perspective, and I'd like to offer you this new point of view as well, from a group of women who were divinely connected to create this project for *you*.

You see, these women don't see the state of the world as a lost cause. Not these women. They instead look through the lens of love and see each moment in life as an opportunity to shine, support, give back and make a difference.

The authors within this collection have opened their hearts and souls in the pages ahead, and have given of themselves with a fearless vulnerability in the hopes that their words, stories and experiences will touch someone, anyone. They didn't set out to change the world with this project, although they do believe it is possible, the optimists that they are! They set out to touch one heart, one soul, and to show you that one random act of kindness—no matter how small—can create a ripple, and that ripple can create a wave.

I'm blessed to have the honor of compiling this book for these talented writers, and in talking with them I've felt such deep admiration for their insight and integrity. While working on this project, I found one theme seems to prevail: peace is an inside job; peace starts from within.

Each author contained in this collection does her part to share her journey, and in so doing, offers hope, despite the sadness that seems to be overshadowing our planet. These women don't see the world as hopeless. These authors look at the world and want to make it better, and they have given of themselves graciously with the sole intention of spreading love and peace to the world. If they can touch even one heart that can resonate with their journey, or one soul who is enlightened by their insights, they will have succeeded. Their mission is so simple, yet so powerful. They set out to do their part to spread love and inspiration, but more importantly, they know that starts with themselves. It begins at home, in solitude, by doing the inner work. And then, once their vibration is raised, they can shine their light upon the world, and in turn, the light of the world will shine a little brighter.

When I founded Spiritual Writers Network back in 2012, my mission was to offer a stage for the writers, healers, artists and lightworkers of the world to raise the world's vibration through love and inspiration, one word at a time. Over time, I began to attract those who had a calling to share their messages, and my vision expanded through my company, Transcendent Publishing, which allowed me to broaden the stage for those talented souls and offer an outlet for their voices to be heard. But they are the heroes, not me. They are the ones who split themselves open and give of themselves so freely, in hopes that their stories will touch someone, anyone, and if that goal is met, their mission will be complete. And that is our intention for this project and all the chapters that grace its pages. If this book reaches just one soul, our work will have purpose, and if it spreads hope to the masses, then we are blessed.

So I ask again, what can *you* do to create peace and love in our world? I encourage you to keep that in mind as you read through the pages ahead, through the writings these brave women have shared so openly with you.

Ladies and gentleman, it is my pleasure to bring you *The Peacemakers.* May we join together to shine light upon the darkness, and do our part to spread that light and love to the world.

~ Shanda Trofe

www.ShandaTrofe.com

Shanda Trofe is the bestselling author of *Authorpreneur: How to Build an Empire and Become the AUTHOR-ity in Your Business*, and *Write from the Heart.* She is the Founder of Spiritual Writers Network, a community of over 3,000 writers and authors, and President & CEO of Transcendent Publishing. Aptly named the Authorpreneur Mentor, Shanda aims to educate aspiring authors not only on the business of writing and publishing but also on how to grow an empire based on the core concepts of their published work.

In addition to working with writers and aspiring authors, Shanda is a certified Mind, Body and Spirit Practitioner, Angel Therapy Practitioner, and Spiritual Life Coach. She believes by incorporating spiritual practices into her business, she can better serve her clients and lead them toward success.

CHAPTER

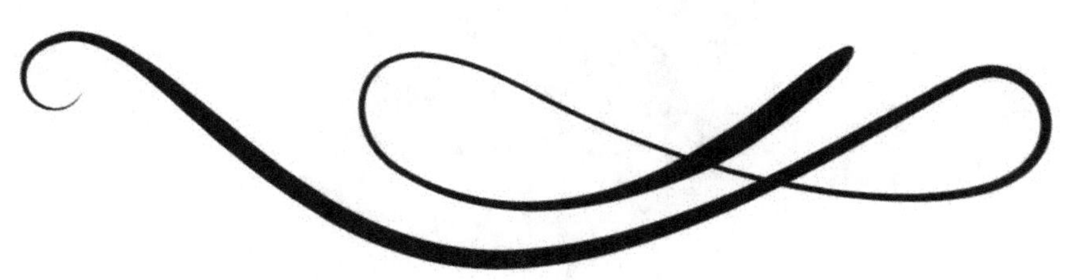

Let it Shine, Let it Shine, Let it Shine

KRISTA GAWRONSKI

Meet **Krista Gawronski**. She is an old friend to The Spiritual Writers Network. She has contributed to the success of other beautiful compilations, ***Finding Our Wings,*** and ***The Light Within.*** Her writing style captures the human spirit and challenges her readers to seek out their spiritual purpose and passion for charity. Every passage she writes has some reference to everyday people carrying out their highest good. One of her greatest accomplishments has been the release of her own story, ***"Soul Purpose…Finding the Courage to Fly."*** It is a heart-shaped novel that documents the universal desire to serve and love. She highlights courage and heroism and records the experience of starting a successful nonprofit called, *The Fabulous Women of Sonoma County,* in her small town of *Petaluma, Ca.*

The chapter in this peacemaker book is an excerpt from her soon-to-be-released project, ***"Be Good."*** Expect Krista to stretch your vision for humanity and challenge you to adopt a small ritual of service into your life. Krista believes that our capacity for love is so great that it is meant to be shared. She inspires her readers to turn their charitable dreams into a lifestyle. Her philosophy will engage your soul and awaken a deeper passion for giving. Best of all, you can get started immediately. To connect with Krista or learn more about her philanthropic story, please see, www.soulpurposecouragetofly.com

DEDICATION

Dedicated to my sons, Frank and Vince Gawronski. May you realize your full potential to love and serve the world. It will never be easy, but it will always be worth it. Everything that truly matters starts and ends with the heart. My love for you is unconditional, and I will always support you to carry out your greatest dreams and highest good. I'm proud to be your mama.

Let it Shine, Let it Shine, Let it Shine

KRISTA GAWRONSKI

How many times have we heard the phrase, "You can't change the world?" Well, I've never bought into that cynicism. I am that crazy woman who believes she can. I suppose I can track some of that optimism all the way back to my childhood. Some of my fondest memories are from when I was a little girl attending Catholic school. I can remember sitting in the pews of St. Gabriel Church, singing songs with Sister Kathy. She was the "Fun Nun" because she had a guitar and she wore running shoes with her habit. If I close my eyes now I can vividly recall everything about my younger self and that joyful little girl sitting in church.

Her hair was sandy blond pulled back in a ponytail, and she had brown freckles all over her face. She wore a blue plaid skirt with a pressed white blouse and round collar. She had black patent leather shoes that her mom picked up at the thrift store, and she wore white socks pulled up to her knees. She was cooperative and happy and kept her hands neatly folded on her lap. Yes, I can still hear her belting out the lyrics to her favorite church hymn, "This little light of mine, I'm gonna let it shine. This little light of mine, I'm gonna let it shine. This little light of mine, I'm gonna let it shine, let it shine, let it shine, let it shine!"

That little girl had self-confidence; she had a joy about her that she could neither harness nor articulate. She adored being around people, and she already knew that she loved life. She didn't care what others thought of her, and it really didn't matter how good or how bad her singing was, either. She was bright and unapologetic. I think she even knew back then that she would have a voice for peace and a message of love. It was clear from the very start that she was quite determined, and there was simply no telling her that she wasn't going to shine bright in this world.

I suppose we could all venture down memory lane and come up with some reflection from our youth when we felt joyful, courageous, and invincible. I think it was a magical time for us because we could exaggerate our love and celebrate our dreams. Yes, I can fondly look back at my youth and appreciate how much easier everything seemed to be. We were uninhibited, we wore clothes that didn't match, we were spontaneous with our hugs, and we loved everybody…just because. There was little pressure to have everything figured out and it was okay to be curious, quirky, and silly. Now that I'm an adult, I'm realizing that a harsh reality can set in. Some of us will become grumpier, and more intolerant, impatient, and unforgiving the older we get.

Every day each of us is faced with societal pressure to "Hurry up and show something for your life!" It has put many of us on edge, and it has also brought a frenzy of chaos along with it. We've become more competitive and judgmental, and we are much more divided socially, economically, and politically. Sadly, we are taking way less time to get to know one another. We are also spending less time getting to know ourselves. We often say that children have a lot to learn from adults. For the sake of this "Peacemaker Book," I would say we have a lot to learn from children. They have the best philosophy and vantage point for life because they view everything through the filter of their hearts. They are simple, authentic, and inclusive. They do not care about status or materialism. Children are optimistic and hopeful, and they recognize the need for hugs, holding hands, and story-time. Do you remember what that was like for you?

Most people report that their childhood held an amazing gift because there was enthusiastic love everywhere. Children marvel over everything. They use words like, **AMAZING, BEAUTIFUL**, and **MAGICAL,** all the time. Isn't it fascinating how children are determined to find things in common with everyone instead of focusing on all the differences that set them apart? So, why does any of that goodness have to change? Why does our view of the world have to become more cynical with time? Just because we grow older doesn't mean that we must abandon our playful spirit or our universal dreams for equality and love. In fact, I believe that we can still do everything that our younger selves ever dreamed possible.

I'm a little wiser than that little girl in church. I am 46 and I no longer believe in Santa. I must admit, the nightly news disturbs me, and the chaos and the division in the world sadden me. BUT guess what? *I STILL WANT TO SHINE!* I still want to carry out my highest good, and I refuse to let age or our fast-moving society determine my worth, my vision, or my path for love. I will not settle into some dismal reality that accepts violence, racism, materialism and suffering. Nope, I will not go along for the ride and abandon my values or my utopia. Despite the fact that the world would like for me to adopt Kim Kardashian as my hero, I will seek my highest good by following other courageous teachers like Martin Luther King, Princess Diana, Gandhi, Maya Angelou, Mother Teresa, and Nelson Mandela. Now, they were the true peacemakers, because they understood that we rise by lifting others. Perhaps we will always compete with the crazy antics of the world, the media influences, and commercialism, but we must remember that life is **NOT** a reality show, and our humanity, integrity, and stability are on the line.

Every author in this book has some grand hope that this conversation about peace will prompt you to reflect on your innocence, your attitude toward people, and your contribution toward peace. If it is a new discussion for you then it may help to close your eyes and ask yourself if you feel safe and comfortable in the world. Yes, please take a moment to think about how the energy of your environment affects your spirit. Are you more inclined to seek out trauma in everything and broadcast sadness and violence, or do you focus on stories of compassion and goodwill? In your reflection you will learn a lot about what you stand for and the vibration that you bring to your life and relationships.

It is not uncommon for people to feel like life is happening to them. However, **LOVE** is an action and we are much more powerful than we give ourselves credit for. Your participation and your heightened awareness of peace and kindness **CAN** change the world. If we allow ourselves to see the goodness around us and commit to fearless acts of compassion, then we can start a life-changing movement. Yes, it can start small. We can start with opening doors, shaking hands, sending cards, and baking casseroles for sick people. Once you make the decision to love and become an instrument for peace, then the entire world around you will begin to change. Lovely human beings are doing extraordinary things every day to promote compassion, unity, and goodwill. Wouldn't it be nice if every person on the planet could literally stop what they're doing and declare love as their highest priority and pledge themselves for peace?

Yes, that would be phenomenal…but it's also next to impossible. I suppose it would take some miracle from the Universe. But here is the better news…**YOU can do it!** You do not need anyone else to hold your hand. This book is a tool for your life. It will strengthen your confidence, restore your hope, and stimulate philanthropic ideas on how you can serve your community. It doesn't matter how old you are, what has happened in your life, or that other people may not join you. It is about your singular decision to carry out your highest good and shine. It's true; I am a bit of an optimist and romantic. I want generosity, courage, and bravery to matter! For that reason, I will not wait for anyone. I'm committed to drawing strength from my creator, like that little girl sitting in church. There's a lovely quote that captures the essence and power of kindness. It is by Desmond TuTu. It will support you in your daily habit to express love, serve others, and unite the people around you. *"Do your little bit of good. It's those little bits of good put together that overwhelm the world."*

My prayer is that this theme for peace and kindness resonates with you. I have always believed that love and compassion can make everything better, and I'm slightly disappointed when society caves in to negative behavior. Yes, we may not be able to fully protect ourselves from cruel people, unexpected hardships, death or tragedy. We do not have control over other people and how they behave. However, we do have some choice in how we personally respond to the greater world and how we conduct ourselves in our homes, at our jobs, in our relationships, and in our communities. I suppose I am simply asking you not to give up on love!

One of my all-time favorite movies has to be ***Love Actually***. The movie opens in Heathrow Airport where people are coming through the terminal to be welcomed by loved ones. The segment highlights people from all different nationalities and ages embracing one another, laughing, smiling, crying, kissing, and holding on to one another tightly. The actor, Hugh Grant, commentates the moment by saying, *"Whenever I get gloomy about the state of the world, I think about the arrivals gate at Heathrow Airport. General opinion is starting to make out that we live in a world of hatred and greed. BUT I don't see that. It seems to me that love is everywhere. Often, it's not particularly dignified or newsworthy, but it's always there...fathers and sons, mothers and daughters, husbands and wives, boyfriends, girlfriends, old friends.... When the planes hit the twin towers as far as I know none of the phone calls from the people inside were messages of* *hate or revenge. They were all messages of love. If you look for it, I have a sneaky feeling you'll find that love actually is all around."*

I have watched ***Love Actually*** over and over. It brings me to tears every single time I see it because I can feel the emotional gravity of that scene. It is based on the undeniable thread and universal wisdom that unites us…LOVE. Every one of us has a profound capacity to give, and this movie clip reminds me that we already have everything we need to live a beautiful and fulfilling life. It also highlights the raw emotion and pure goodness that comes from our authentic expression. It is true; we are more alike than different. Our desire to love and be loved makes us the same no matter who we are, no matter how old we are, no matter where we come from, and no matter what our exterior shell looks like. Perhaps, if we can remember this incredible wisdom, then our walls would come down a little easier, our hearts would open up just a little more, and the nature of the world would be a little more peaceful.

It is true; sometimes our greater world has mixed up their priorities. I have asked myself a few times over, "Are you okay with the state of the world? And if you aren't, what are you doing to make it better?" The truth is some people have become numb and unresponsive and a few people have joined the chaos. I'm pretty confident that you've chosen a different path in your journey because you've selected a book with a title for peace. The sheer fact that you're brave enough to take in the wisdom of these chapters tells me that you care about the people around you and the community you live in. Yes, I'm quite confident that you are a **"Kindness Warrior,"** and you are taking brave steps in your life to promote love, tolerance, charity, and compassion. I suppose it might sound a little dramatic to refer to you as a "Kindness Warrior," but I can think of no better term in today's world to describe the spirit needed to combat the negativity and ugly chaos. If you can do something small and extraordinary every single day then you will become a part of the solution. I can assure you that society and the Universe are begging us to get involved. Don't worry, you are not being asked to solve the greater perils of the world. Your assignment is much easier. You are just being asked to do something loving that your younger self will thank you for.

It's funny that we often challenge ourselves to think about the wisdom we would share with our younger selves. However, for the purpose of today's lesson, I think we should draw our finest advice from our younger selves. Let us do more from our hearts to carry out our highest good and realize our capacity to love one another, solve problems, and heal wounds. When we give ourselves permission to love and serve the world, another level of spirituality develops. Life takes on the most profound meaning, and our life story becomes more meaningful. Yes, for every child who is brave enough to share their dream to make the world a better place, we should encourage their heart's desire, because one day we will become old enough and strong enough to fulfill that destiny. May we honor the journey and realize our greatest potential, and together let us do everything humanly possible to shine, shine, shine!

CHAPTER

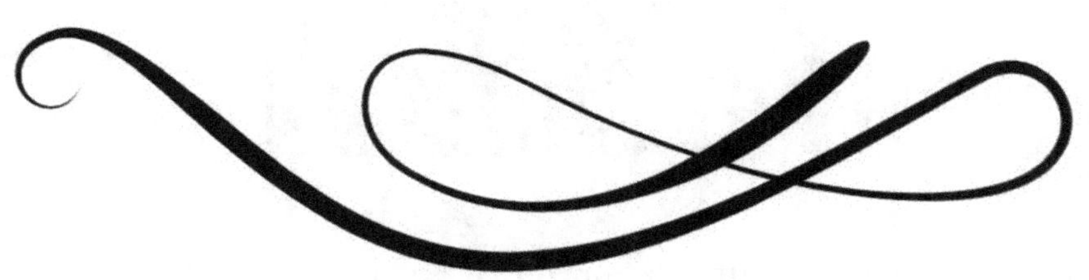

Spreading Peace by Restoring Self-Love

MISTY PROFFITT-THOMPSON

Misty Proffitt-Thompson is a Certified Angel Card Reader and a Mind, Body, Spirit Practitioner who owns the Spiritual-based business, Mystified Enlightenment. She conducts workshops on Angels and is currently creating course material on forgiveness, following your intuition, spiritual guidance and the use of essential oils. She also reads Angel Cards for her clients, which offers positive help on their life path. Misty is in the process of writing a book about the tragic death of her sister and the spiritual journey between the two of them.

Connect with Misty

Email: contact@mistymthompson.com

Website: www.mistymthompson.com

Social Media: www.facebook.com/mystifiedenlightenment

ACKNOWLEDGEMENTS

I am grateful for the support of my family: my husband, Thomas; my children, Brittany, Jacob, Joshua, and Tuesday; and my grandchildren, Josiah, Damian, Ashton, and Caleb. I also acknowledge my mom, Norma Rhodes, who has suffered so much in her life, including the most devastating loss, the death of my younger sister, Stephanie, in 1993. Each of them have believed in me and helped me during this journey to find my calling. Words cannot express how much I love you all and appreciate you. I also acknowledge my mentors, Sunny Dawn Johnston, Shanda Trofe, and The Psychic Twins. Thank you all for your positive, spiritual and energetic support.

DEDICATION

I am dedicating this entire book and this chapter to my children. Thank you for being my teachers in this experience we call life. May the peace inside you flourish and expand to those around you. I love you all.

Spreading Peace by Restoring Self-Love

MISTY PROFFITT-THOMPSON

The world around us now is much different than it was when I was younger in the 70s and 80s. While I was growing up, the thought of one person making a difference in this world by disseminating peace seemed both ridiculous and impossible, to say the least. As I received knowledge that allowed me to blossom, as my spiritual side started to flourish, and as my life in this realm gave me more experience, I began to realize that being a peacemaker didn't mean the goal was to conquer the enemy. It meant that I should let my spirituality shine, follow my inner guidance, and trust that God and the Angels would send to me those people I could help from a place of love. That is doing my part.

I believe that restoring our self-love is one of the most important steps we can take in order to show peace in this world. We all at one time have had the experience of showing love to ourselves and not feeling guilty about it. As babies, we were happy and content as long as our basic needs were met. We giggled, played, explored, and were close to our Creator. As we grew, circumstances and situations occurred that impacted our spirit, and as a result we lost that self-love. As humans growing older, we all have experienced something that has damaged our self-esteem and the ability to love ourselves. I believe that this lack of self-love has caused the peace of the world to suffer as well. What we give we receive, and if we are sending out low-vibration, dense energies like hatred, jealousy, bitterness and guilt because that is what we are feeling inside, we have a tendency to not only receive that back ourselves, but that thinking sends out negativity into the world as well. As a result, the peace of all living things will eventually be diminished.

There are several things one can do to restore self-love. The steps are easy once you decide to fully let go of your control. The difficult part is finding one area of interest that resonates with your true self. As different as every person is in their personality traits, needs, likes and dislikes, they can discover many diverse areas that will help with the restoration of one's love and peace within. This is where you listen to that nudge, that gut-feeling telling you how you can restore your self-love. I have given you some exercises below that continue to help me and others.

I have found that one of the greatest ways to restore self-love is to forgive. This means forgiveness for those who have wronged you and, most importantly, forgiveness of yourself. Many times the acts that need to be forgiven are really not about you. When people have committed negative attacks towards you, most of the time it is a reflection of their own personal issues. Unfortunately, they are taking out their frustrations on the wrong person. Forgiveness is more for you, so you can release those negative emotions due to your lack of forgiveness. Hanging on to those lower, negative, dense emotions does nothing for you but bring you down.

Forgiveness of yourself is also necessary for past choices you have made. Holding on to guilt and shame for those choices will prevent you from taking the journey of peace and love for yourself. We all have made and will continue to make mistakes and you have to believe that you did the best you could with the information you had at the time. We are older and wiser now and recognize that you would not make those same decisions now. Put down on paper those feelings you have involving guilt, which is from doing a bad thing, and shame, which is from believing that you are a bad person, and burn that paper, offering it up into the universe. That is a great way to release these dark feelings from your head and heart and allow God to handle those human emotional setbacks. Start small and work your way up. It is likely true that guilt and shame will not reveal themselves overnight, so please be patient. Start the process and look back upon your progress every six months or so to see how far you have come. When you believe that you are capable of releasing those dense negative vibrations, the process will begin to go deeper. As you continue to keep up with this practice, you will start to see that the self-love you deserve is beginning its restoration.

Working on gratitude is another tool that can be beneficial. I personally keep a Gratitude Jar. When I am feeling joyful, I express that feeling and what brought it about on a piece of paper and put it in my jar. When I am feeling down, I re-read those pieces of paper and almost immediately, I am brought back to that joyful place. You can also place a hand on your heart while saying thank you. This is a way to express to the Universe that you are grateful and joyful for those small gifts in life, even if you do not completely believe it at the time. Showing appreciation for what you have will in turn bring others to appreciate you. That will build your confidence and since your confidence will be restored, so will a love for yourself. Offering praise and complimenting others will find its way back to you.

Another way to cultivate your inner peace is to journal. Write all of those dense emotions (anger, jealousy, hate, guilt, shame) you are feeling down on a piece of paper. Include the people involved, the situation, and express all of your feelings. Again, when you get that out and onto paper, you will be able to rid yourself of it. As I suggested earlier, burning the paper is even more effective. When you do that you are getting those unhappy elements out of your mind and heart, allowing the universe to take those emotions. You can also just write your general feelings of the day. Journaling doesn't always have to be negative. Describing those occurrences that happened during the day that made you laugh, smile, or reminded you of what gave you joy will also bring happiness and ultimately self-love.

Another option is using affirmations. Standing in front of a mirror and repeating positive statements will help you regain your self-love and find peace within. In our head we seem to replay the negative things we believe about ourselves. The more you focus on those, the more you will begin to accept them and this will damage our self-love and, ultimately, our peace. We all deserve to be happy; it is our God-given right. We all have a spark of light in us because we are a creation of God. It is important to see ourselves and others we encounter the way God and the Angels do, with unconditional love. Stating positive affirmations will change your mind-set for the better. Offering praise and complimenting others will bring those same benefits to you.

I have come to realize that I cannot defeat the enemy in its entirety. But I can do my part to help those around me. We are all trying to find our way in this life. We cannot move forward unless our self-love is nurtured and supported so growth and expansion can occur. Once self-love is achieved, peace will advance within us, and like a wildfire it will spread quickly and fiercely, bringing peace to the world.

CHAPTER

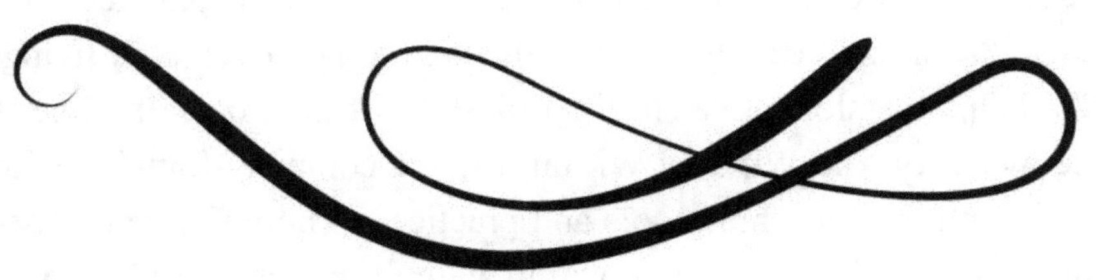

Finding Compassion in all the Right Places

KATE SHIPP

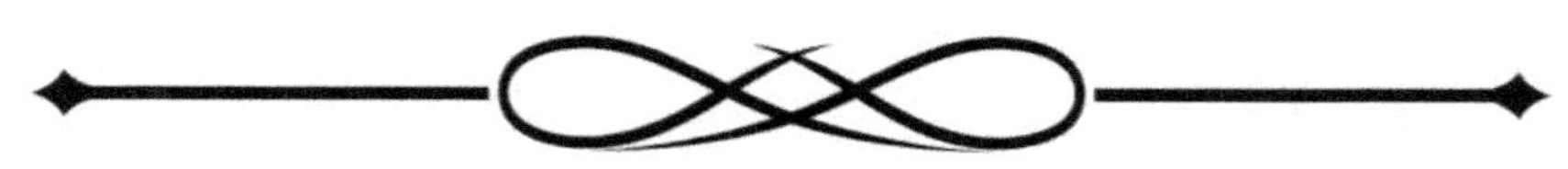

Kate Shipp is a Spiritual Mentor who uses her intuitive gifts combined with embodied mindfulness practices and energy healing to reveal the path to heart-centered living. She helps transform lives to the fullest expression of Self. Kate is the owner of The Window Within, LLC, a company founded with the intention of teaching tools and practices to help you remember the radiant light that shines within your heart, and to show you how to allow that light to be your guide in daily life. She is deeply passionate about blending science and spirituality to create an understanding of Oneness.

Kate works with clients privately, guides classes and retreats, and mentors in Spiritually Embodied Living, a program she created to teach people to remember they are the integration of spirit and humanity in one. By learning to merge body, mind, heart, and spirit, one is able to live a divinely guided, love-based life. Her work is often referred to as intuitive, transformational, healing, unveiling, compassionate, and a way of finding vulnerability. Her clients refer to her as an intuitive healer, a shadow-excavator, a mindful sage, a gentle soul, and a lighthouse.

Kate is a 500ERYT, with over 1500 hours in formal yoga training. She holds certifications in Yoga, Phoenix Rising Yoga Therapy, and Yoga Nidra. She is a Reiki Master Teacher, a Psychic Medium, and a certified Mind, Body, Spirit Practitioner.

She teaches the Transformational Yoga Coaching program at The Southwest Institute of Healing Arts in Tempe, AZ. She holds a B.S. in Marketing from Arizona State University.

Connect with Kate

Email: kateshippyoga@gmail.com
Website: www.thewindowwithin.com
Social Media: Facebook.com/thewindowwithin

ACKNOWLEDGEMENT

I am deeply grateful to my husband, Eric, and my children, Connor and Makena. Their support, love, and encouragement have helped me to find the true me, and to let my light shine in bigger and better ways. To my family and friends, thank you all for your love, for your willingness to stand by my side, for your help in times of struggle, and for your support in pursuing my dreams. To my clients, you are the reason I do what I do. I am forever grateful for your courage and vulnerability to go deep-sea diving with me on this journey to self-love.

DEDICATION

This chapter is dedicated to all of my teachers and mentors who have shared with me their journeys, their sufferings, their joys, their successes, and guide me back to my heart each and every day. Your wisdom, teachings, and openness to being authentic with me have made a lasting impression at the core of who I am. I thank you all for your willingness to be seen, to be vulnerable, and to be a guide I can walk with on this path. Namaste.

Finding Compassion in All the Right Places

KATE SHIPP

May you find peace in your heart.

May you find joy in your eyes.

May you find passion in your belly.

May you find light in your smile.

May you find love is life.

There comes a time in your life when you realize that nothing will ever be the same again. Those moments may come unexpectedly or perhaps they are planned; the birth of a child, the death of a loved one, an illness, a wedding, a college acceptance letter, a house fire, a promotion, a simple, 'Hello.' As these life-altering moments arise, you know, you feel within your entire being that everything will be different.

The heart quickens, the body may freeze, the mind becomes still or even chaotic, the breath is breathless. Are you in your body or do you feel like you are floating? Are you aware of your feet on the Earth or are you lost in the clouds, unable to be in the moment because it feels like something has come crashing into your heart and you are not quite sure what to do with it?

Those times in life when we feel knocked over, when we feel joyfully elated, when we confront the unknown, I call those times, The Pause. It reminds me of when a song ends on the radio or your iPod is on shuffle and there is that little place of silence. That stillness. You wonder what's coming next. Do you ever listen to the silence of the pause or do you quickly hit next, or even try to guess what is coming? This is the space between what was and what will be.

Sometimes that pause can last only a few seconds, and sometimes that pause can last years. This pause has the ability to propel us forward into the light of the new, or spiral us down into the depths of the shadows as we prepare for a glorious rebirth. No matter how long that pause remains, it is important to have practices we can perform to bring ourselves back to center, into a place of self-compassion.

One of the greatest gifts we can give ourselves is the gift of compassion. Compassion allows us to meet ourselves where we are without judgment, expectation, or shame for what we are experiencing; it is the gift of true presence. In this place of presence is where peace resides and where you can at last begin to relax and settle into that space of light within your heart. That place where the happenings of the outside world slow, where noises, emotions, sensations, and thoughts fade. In that space of pause, of grace, that is where you find the energy that will heal your heart, heal the world. This is where love resides.

Most of the time I see people looking to outside sources of wisdom for help. I am a big supporter of reaching out, but I also firmly believe in our own inherent wisdom that resides within us all! There is a source of guidance that is always available to us; a vast expanse of energy that holds the very essence of who we are: OUR BODY!

The body does not lie. It is your breathing source of Divine guidance that holds the keys to deep healing. The mind may create stories about what is happening in the body but the body only speaks the truth. It knows no other way. It stores the experiences of our lives in our very cells. It responds to life and is able to heal itself when provided with the right conditions. When passing through the unknown, by tuning into your body, you are accessing intuitive wisdom to gain clarity, calm, and guidance.

Here are some simple ways to come into a place of self-compassion. They all work. Trust me. Once you are in that moment of stillness, where only love lives, from that place, the pause, all becomes clear.

Simple Practices to Invoke Self-Compassion

1. When faced with the unknown, one of the quickest ways to bring yourself back to center is through your breath. Here is one simple breath practice that connects, body, mind, and spirit. Bring your left hand to your heart and your right hand to your abdomen. Feel your heartbeat under your left hand and the gentle rhythm of your breath under your right hand. As you inhale, expand your belly into your hand then carry the breath into your heart. Silently say to yourself, I AM. As you exhale, allow your heart to slow and your belly to contract back to your spine. Silently say to yourself, LOVE. Repeat until you feel a shift in your energy. It will feel calmer, lighter and more at peace.
2. If you feel like the connection to your body has diminished, or you feel a brain fog coming over you, here is an offering that will help reaffirm your connection to grounding energy and restore a sense of control and power. Stand up. Bring your feet to hip distance, toes facing forward. Be sure to have a slight bend at the knees. Press the entire surface of your feet into the ground and feel the connection to the earth beneath you. Now, engage your thighs by lifting your knees. Pull your navel point in and slightly up. Allow your shoulders to relax back, and lift the crown of your head toward the sky, as if a string was pulling up on the top of your head. Close your eyes and begin to breathe consciously. On the inhale silently state, I AM. On the exhale silently state, STRONG. Repeat this until you

feel a deep connection go through you, grounding you as it passes through your legs, and an opening comes deep within, as it enters into your heart.

3. Take out a piece of paper and list the numbers 1-5. Answer these five questions:

    1. What happened? Be specific

    2. What am I experiencing now? Be specific.

    3. What part of my body is most showing up in this very moment?

    4. Tune into that part of the body and ask: What do I need to know? Listen for a response. It will come. It may just not be what you expect to hear.

    5. What do I need to do to help myself find more compassion and love in this situation? Listen to your body.

4. Experience a sensory walk in Nature. Take yourself outside. Whether that be in your backyard, to a park, or anywhere else outside. If you feel the need to have your phone, please put it away. As you begin to walk, become aware of all of your senses. What are you noticing? List 5 things you see. What are you feeling? List 5 things that you feel. For example, your legs moving, the wind in your hair, the sun on your skin. Listen to the sounds all around and list 5 things that you hear. Inhale deeply and list 5 scents that you smell. This may take a little longer but stick with it. Finally, find a tree, a rock, a bush, a flower, and touch it. Look at it with open eyes and take 5 slow deep breaths. Continue walking for 10 minutes or longer as you engage all your senses in this experience. Allow yourself to be completely present to your place in nature.

5. Body Gratitude Practice. Begin by lying down comfortably. Close your eyes. You will be going through each body part giving gratitude for all your

> body does for you every day. Begin with your feet. Silently stating, I am grateful for my toes. I am grateful for my feet. I am grateful for my ankles. I am grateful for my shins and calves. I am grateful for my knees. I am grateful for my thighs. I am grateful for my hips. I am grateful for my pelvis. I am grateful for my buttocks. I am grateful for my abdomen. I am grateful for my chest. I am grateful for my shoulders. I am grateful for my upper arms. I am grateful for my lower arms. I am grateful for my hands. I am grateful for my fingers. I am grateful for my elbows. I am grateful for my collarbones. I am grateful for my throat. I am grateful for my ears. I am grateful for my lips. I am grateful for my teeth and tongue. I am grateful for my nose. I am grateful for my eyes. I am grateful for my forehead. I am grateful for my hair. I am grateful for my head. I am grateful for my neck. I am grateful for my shoulder blades. I am grateful for my upper back. I am grateful for my lower back. I am grateful for my whole spinal cord. I am grateful for my skin, my organs, my nerves, my glands, my heart, my brain. I am grateful for my breath that brings life into this magnificent body. I am grateful for all my body allows me to do each and every day. Body, I thank you!

As we learn to hold a sacred space for ourselves, to give ourselves the love and compassion that our hearts so deeply desire, we are better able to hold that space for others. Through the gifts of compassion, grace, and love, we can heal the wounds of the past, we can embrace the joys of daily life, and we can thrive in a world of love and peace. It all begins by loving yourself, wholly and completely, just at you are, in every moment. Remember that when life presents you with a pause, you decide what you will create from that moment. You alone can create a shift in energy that brings this world closer to Oneness.

CHAPTER

Finding Peace within the Pieces

MELISSA KIM CORTER

Melissa Kim Corter is the creator of Earth Moon Medicine, Soul Artistry™ and is a Certified Hypnotherapist and Shamanic practitioner certified in Elemental Space Clearing™, Gateway Dreaming™, and over 20 other healing modalities. She helps clients release fear & clear away the emotional clutter from their life experiences. Through various modalities coupled with her heightened intuition, she connects with your spirit for expanded truth and guidance on how to shift limiting beliefs. The earth, moon, and elements have been a channel for deeper levels of healing and connection for Melissa, stirring a passion within her to teach others to embrace the natural world.

One of her renowned gifts is taking people into deep levels of relaxation through guided meditations and Hypnotherapy, projecting her voice to take you on a peaceful and transformational soul journey.

Melissa lives in Sedona, Arizona with her two fur-babies, husband of thirteen years and their amazing son. She works with private clients, teaches classes online and hosts workshops and retreat all over the country and beyond.

Connect with Melissa:

Art of Abundance FREE:
www.facebook.com/groups/artofabundance/

Melissa Corter- Soul Artist:
www.facebook.com/melissacortersoulartist/

Website: www.melissacorter.com

ACKNOWLEDGEMENT

To Denise, you have inspired me to believe in magic, to trust deeply in my spirit, and to start before you are ready!
I love you dearly.

DEDICATION

To my husband Kristopher...thank you for walking me through the fear and reminding me, in my own power, to create a new story.

Finding Peace within the Pieces

MELISSA KIM CORTER

I sat in meditation, waiting for the answer to float to the surface of my awareness, as it often will. I entered into this meditation intentionally to discover the contents of this writing, eager to find the possibilities it could contain. After a short while, I felt called to talk about a particular part of my journey into healing. This came as a shock, since my intention was to share about peace and how to be a Peacemaker in this world. After sitting with this a few moments longer, the connection started to make more sense. I continued holding the intention of peace, and what came to mind was, "A peacemaker in life is first and foremost a piece-maker."

Imagine collecting all the threads of a tapestry, various colors and lengths, weaving them into form, to reveal a beautiful mandala of color and depth… now imagine that tapestry representing all of your life experiences. This is similar to my own journey. A sojourn of self love, learning to embrace the various threads of my being, instead of rejecting them.

As a young adult, starting out in the healing arts industry over 15+ years ago, I had a desire to help and heal others. Although my intentions were pure, and I was filled with compassion, I was helping others from a place of lack, neglecting my own needs. It wasn't until I began my own healing journey that all of the pieces came in, reflecting back to me the layers of work that I needed to do. Every time I set out to shift an experience, to cultivate forgiveness and move through fear, I reclaimed another aspect of myself.

I had heard of terms such as the wounded healer, yet it wasn't until shining a light into my own shadow that I recognized my need for approval and validation. Each person I worked with immensely enjoyed our time and received great benefit, yet I was constantly craving something new, something different. I wasn't coming from a place of wholeness; I was operating from the level of ego, and a place of emptiness. Trying to fill the void through my work and living vicariously through other people's healing created a false sense of empowerment. I was good at it, and my business started to expand with more and more clients.

One day a client I had been working with for a few months asked me the same question she continued asking me each month, and it hit me like a ton of bricks. She was coming to me for answers, instead of tapping in to her own answers. She wanted me to tell her what she wanted to hear, not how she could shift the energy of the situation. Feeling defeated, I walked away from my business and picked up my camera for a creative outlet to distract me from my pain and frustration. I made a decision by declaring I would no longer work with people who were seeking answers from their own level of lack.

Now hear me clearly, this is not a judgment of that beautiful client; in fact, she was a mirror and a teacher for me. This experience with her opened my eyes and my heart. In all the time I spent training with shamans and psychics, teachers and mentors, one of my greatest lessons was revealed from this beautiful soul through nothing more than her innocent moment of inquiry.

My healing quest continued to unfold after my having invoked a different capacity within which to work. I formed a new alliance with myself and my clients as the process became more internal. I began working with the pieces of myself and my being that I had been trying to neglect, hide, and cut out. My attention shifted, and I started traveling inward, learning to love all of the orphaned parts of my being. Each time I recalled my energy, and healed one of these aspects, a new evidence of wholeness entered into my life. After a few years of this journey, I felt secure enough within myself to work with clients once again. This time I reminded them that they are their own peacemaker, and they have every tool they need to manifest that within their own mind and heart. Being present with "what is" became the magic in creating peace.

Being a peacemaker shifted from wanting to fix broken things and people (the old language of my ego), to reminding people of their wholeness. We have lots of work to do and lots of lessons to learn, but despite that, we can still choose to operate from a place of peace. It is a choice in every moment, choosing peace or choosing something else. We are going to have challenging moments when it is harder to choose peace, especially when it feels like it is locked in a vault, always out of reach. This is nothing more than the ego's desire to create separation; another aspect we each have that still deserves love.

Our outer world begins to reflect peace when it is first cultivated inside. To be a true peacemaker in this world we first have to start with ourselves, examining every opportunity for self-love, compassion, and forgiveness. Imagining these three as pieces, and fitting them into the puzzle of who we are, is one of the first steps to true inner peace.

We can experience tragedy, loss, and anger, and still make grounded choices in how we respond to what is happening within and around us. Taking ownership of emotions, reactions, and feelings is empowering; oftentimes, it gives permission to others to do the same. Many of us are unknowingly waiting for someone to open a door within us. It is safe and it is necessary to have the desire to open the door yourself. You have the key, your soul knows the pieces you hold, and they are only waiting for your acknowledgment, love and compassion.

Finding your way back to wholeness is not an easy journey, especially when first learning to love who you are. Many of us fear change in our relationships, our careers, and the unknown. On a deeper level there is a part of us that fears not knowing where we will fit in if we were to receive all that we seek and become the person that we are called to be. For some, the discomfort we live with can be more appealing than the discomfort of change. It is within the space of the unknown that magic exists and healing occurs.

If you were to pick one life experience that caused enormous fear and/or even pain, physical, mental or emotional, somewhere within that experience you would find a blessing and a gift. For some of us that gift is resilience, a reminder of how short life is, or discovering your own strength. The blessing that is born from the pain can only be determined by the one who perceives it, as each of us will have a different vantage point or perspective. This is why each of us can experience the same thing and have a completely unique perspective on what happened, a unique response to it, and be uniquely affected by it.

Knowing yourself truly and deeply, having a willingness to discover the hidden aspects of your being is empowering. Many of us are afraid that we will uncover something frightening, something that would push others away, or something that would validate our own fear of being separate from the whole. The truth is there is nothing you are not aware of, or as one of my mentors says, "the soul loves the truth."

It is liberating to release our burdens, the emotional weight we carry from day to day. Creating an opportunity for yourself to unburden, to share, to express, whatever it is you're carrying within your heart, can lift the weight of the world from your shoulders. When you shine a light into the darkness, the darkness cannot hide. When you get comfortable knowing who you are and all of the experiences that helped create the patterns of your being, you begin shifting your choices. You can now choose from a conscious place, deciding on the layers you wish to keep, and the layers you wish to transform. You can embrace the parts of your being that once would have terrified you, and you can release other parts of your being that are no longer serving you.

I feel this is the true work of the peacemaker: somebody is willing to look at all of the pieces, and still focus on the love and potential of that human soul. To look into the darkness and still find the light, to be with those whom everyone else has turned their back on, to become a witness and be mindful that they just haven't found a way yet to love all of their pieces. Witnessing the world from this place makes it hard to contribute to the heaviness. It then feels more in alignment to project love instead of assumptions.

Peacemakers are human and have their own lessons and times of need while finding ways to let the heart guide them. They make peace and harmony a priority, even in times when love is the last thing they want to offer, as it is sometimes the only way to heal.

Peacemakers know how to give, they understand it is about wholeness and truth, not having to be right. Truth can be acceptance in knowing that regardless of what you say, you cannot change how others hear or perceive you; all that matters is that you continue weaving your beautiful tapestry. Trust that the end result will be a magnificent masterpiece all your own. Be the peacekeeper to yourself, and the world will reflect your efforts back to you, over and over. Through cultivating and nurturing your own inner peace, you are creating an invitation for others to do the same.

May you be peaceful, may you be well, may you be happy,
may you be safe, may you awaken to the light of your own being,
may you be free (Metta prayer).

CHAPTER

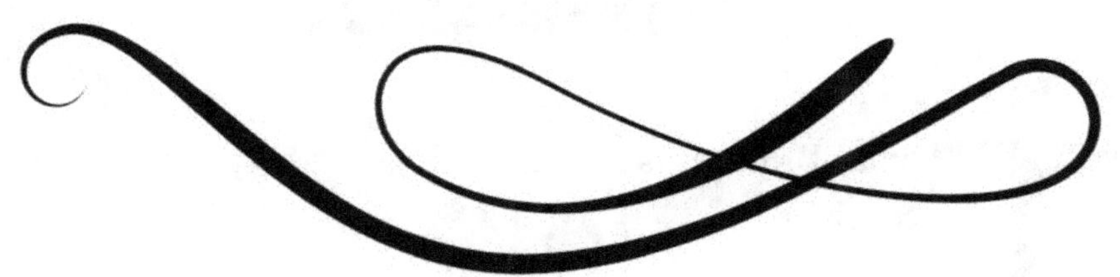

A Little Piece of Peace

TONIA BROWNE

Tonia Browne is a best-selling author, teacher and coach.

As a teacher, Tonia has worked in the United Kingdom and internationally for over twenty years and was an Assistant Head for seven.

Tonia is a strong advocate of inviting fun into our lives and encouraging people to see their world from a new perspective.

Her writing includes coaching strategies tightly interwoven with spiritual insights and personal anecdotes. She has a holistic approach to change and believes in liberating the Indigo Child within each of us.

In addition to her mainstream training as a teacher, Tonia is a Heal Your Life® Workshop Leader, Coach and Business Trainer. She is also a Reiki Master Teacher and has studied Angelic Reiki to teacher level. She has a Diploma in Color Therapy, Life Coaching and Neuro-Linguistic Programming along with a Certification in Counselling Skills and Spiritual Coaching.

Tonia has accepted the help of amazing people along her journey and enjoys returning the favor by assisting others in their development.

She combines her skills in her new book. *Spiritual Seas: Diving into Life* is about her diving adventures, spiritual insights and practical strategies for riding the waves of life.

Connect with Tonia

Website: www.toniabrowne.com

Facebook: Time4T @ facebook.com/Time4Tonia

Twitter: twitter.com/ToniaUae

ACKNOWLEDGEMENT

I would like to acknowledge all who have helped me in my life and all those helping to keep the peace in our world.

DEDICATION

This chapter is dedicated to a peaceful world—within and without.

A Little Piece of Peace

TONIA BROWNE

A New Game at School

"We played a new game at school today," she told me with an odd look on her beautiful six-year-old face.

"Tell me about it," I enquired.

"When the teacher shouts '*down'* we all have to fall to the floor, under the table, and then keep still."

I was perplexed. What was that all about?

"That's a funny game," was my only reply.

"It's in case the bad people come to school," she said, as if confused herself.

I quickly understood. Realising the seriousness of what had just passed between us I asked if she had enjoyed the game.

"No, I didn't. I had Matty's smelly shoes in my face."

I held my nose, wrinkled it and we both laughed.

A Global Closeness

What was happening in the world? When did children have to worry about people invading their schools with the intention of harm? When did people in hospitals and families on outings have to be so vigilant? When did caregivers with prams need to undergo such scrutiny and suspicion at security checks? When did our world become this conflicted? Sadly I had some idea. It was shouted loud from our televisions, printed boldly in our newspapers and it filled our social media.

With global communication, when events happen, we all know about it almost instantly and we almost seem to feel it. It either brings a sense of global closeness and compassion or fear, anger and a need for revenge. As a society we seem to be losing our hope and expectation for peace. It is easy to see why as tragedy after tragedy gains star position on our media platforms. Death, misery, starvation and disaster seem to be everywhere.

Conversations on the streets, on buses and trains are filled with the sounds of people's disbelief over what they have read, heard and seen happening around our world. And it is *our world.* However much we identify with just a piece of it and segregate areas with borders to make it solely ours, we are connected. We hope that if we can close our doors we will be secure. It isn't that simple. We need to find a way to live together peacefully for our world to become safer. We are all part of the human race with hopes and needs, regardless of religious belief or place of birth.

A Little Piece of Peace

In a world that seems so unpredictable and with events that impact us all, it is understandable how many feel insecure. Experiencing depression, confusion, indecision, cancelled holidays, limited budgets, harsh words as well as sleepless nights, many are losing their peace of mind.

But the sun still shines and water still flows. We see children skip through fields of daisies and look for rainbows on showery days. They still play games together, many of which are make-believe. Why spoil their happiness before we must? Why destroy their peace of mind with the madness of our time? As we talk in front of them and as we share our fears, we infringe on their world of innocence and their chance to dream.

We may need to take some action to find resolution in our changing world. But let's do more of what the teacher did when she turned the new school policy of potential invasion into a game. While we still can, and for as long as we can, let's hold on to our peace within, as much for the children's sake as for ourselves. If we can maintain a peace within us maybe we can share it with the world about us.

A calming voice, a soothing phrase, an act of kindness and our faith can help us keep or find our peace, one moment at a time. While others try to incite fear and all it entails, let's be resolute together to hold on to at least a little piece of peace within. And then let it grow. As others have taught us before, we have a choice whether to live in love or fear.

"Darkness cannot drive out darkness; only light can do that. Hate cannot drive out hate; only love can do that."

~ Martin Luther King, Jr.

"Peace is a daily, a weekly, a monthly process, gradually changing opinions, slowly eroding old barriers, quietly building new structures."

~ John F. Kennedy

"The future belongs to those who believe in the beauty of their dreams."

~ Eleanor Roosevelt

Peace of Mind

I hope that peace on Earth is more than just a dream. But while we dream and help make the dream a reality, we can also create a little peace within us through maintaining peace of mind.

This is not always possible but, if you become aware, you will find that some people seem to have more serenity than others. This is not always by disposition or circumstances, but through a deliberate focus. They flexed the peace of mind muscle until it started flexing for itself.

If exhibiting peace and serenity is not your normal response to life, like in many other areas, it will need some action on your part in order to help develop it.

To develop peace of mind, try some of the following ideas and strategies. Find the ones that work best for you and consciously do them until they become an unconscious response:

- Live one moment at a time - don't think too far ahead.
- Take deep and slow breaths, perhaps learning yoga or meditating.
- If you are right you don't always need to prove it.
- Find the silver lining.
- Acknowledge what you have.
- Create a space for you in your day.
- Enjoy the little things in life.
- As far as you can, decide for yourself what you will watch and read - don't get caught up in gossip or fear-mongering.
- Remember, tomorrow offers another chance.
- Understand that life is about change so enjoy as much of what is here while you can.
- Spend time outside and commune with nature - grow flowers, watch the stars, enjoy a sunset and watch the

waves of the sea.

- Be grateful.
- Make friends.
- Help others.
- Forgive.
- Believe in miracles
- and never stop nurturing your piece of peace.

The Peacemakers Within

To the peacemakers and lovers,
to the sisters and brothers,
I hope you find peace on Earth.

To the old and the weak,
and those whose futures seem bleak,
I hope you find peace in your time.

To the teenagers and young,
and to heroes unsung,
I hope you find peace in your world.

To the doctors and teachers,
parents and preachers,
please continue to promote peace on Earth.

But when all's said and done,
let's try to have fun
as we wait for change to arrive.
And while we create reasons to cheer
and pray our paths become clear,
let's continue to be gentle and kind.
By doing so,
I hope we might find,
some
peace of mind.

CHAPTER *Six*

Dreaming into Being

R.D. PETTI

R.D. Petti is a mystic, poet, and debut author of the spiritual fantasy, *Nettie's Tea House: A Tale of the Afterlife*, acclaimed by a Writer's Digest contest judge as "a rewarding tale, meant to be savored." Having earned a B.A. in English Literature and an M.A. in Counseling Psychology, she has been a lifelong student of consciousness, seeking the knowledge and wisdom found in mystery and spiritual traditions. She has served as a mental health counselor, hospice volunteer, and Reiki Master Practitioner.

Ms. Petti resides in Sarasota, Florida. She is a Letters member of the National League of American Pen Women and belongs to the ABC Artisans of Books. One of her poems was recently awarded first place in a Spiritual Writers Network contest and appears in its poetry anthology, *Illuminations of the Soul*. An environmental enthusiast, Ms. Petti supports the Mote Marine Laboratory as a Turtle Patrol volunteer.

Connect with R.D. Petti

Website: www.rdpetti.com

Social Media: www.facebook.com/rdpettiauthor

ACKNOWLEDGEMENTS

With undying gratitude to my children for their unconditional love and belief in me. For that, I am humbled, honored, and forever blessed. Special thanks to the National League of American Pen Women. My professional life has been enriched since joining this distinguished organization of creative women. Many thanks to Kathleen Marusak. You are an awesome editor. And last but not least, heartfelt thanks to light bearers everywhere, including Shanda Trofe, publisher of this book, and its contributing writers. Your compassion lights the way to a more peaceful world.

DEDICATION

To the memory of Robin Hunt: gifted writer, humorist, soul sister. Your earthly lamp was extinguished too soon, but your eternal light continues to shine bright on us. Your compassionate spirit will live on forever in our hearts. Until we meet again, my friend.

Dreaming into Being

R.D. PETTI

Long ago, in the mists of time, there was a girl of pure heart. She lived with her family and their tribe at the edge of the forest. Her grandfather, the patriarch of the tribe, was a mage of immense power and wisdom. He taught her the ways of the forest and shared with her the secrets of the universe before he passed through the veil to the realm of spirit. There he was transformed into the Green Man, a spirit of nature and guardian of the Earth Mother, Gaia. He dwelled in the higher dimensions of the universe, but his essence could be sensed on Earth in every tree, plant, flower, and leaf throughout the green world; his voice, heard whispering on the breeze, in the rustling leaves, and blades of grass.

The girl and her tribe were peace-loving people. They looked with compassion upon the suffering of humanity, to those whose hearts were wounded by violence, hatred, and fear, and, at witnessing these evils, they wept. The heart of the Earth Mother, filled with unconditional love and kindness for all denizens of her planet, was broken. She, too, wept, for the suffering of humanity was beyond what she could endure.

Gaia called upon the assistance of the Green Man, who could hear from on high the cries of sorrow all over the planet. He dedicated himself at once to Gaia's service and asked his assembly of guardians—the nature sprites, devas, and elementals—to journey to the Earth plane with him to help Gaia in her cause to heal the troubled hearts of humanity. The Green Man and the other nature guardians dwelled in a wooded glen he had created in the spirit realm and which was the template for the physical forests beautifying the planet Earth. He summoned the assembly to gather at the megalithic stone circle in the glen.

As he waited for the assembly, the Green Man took strength from the glen, teeming with life and possessing a deep richness. Birds of every color and species sang to him. Bluebells frolicked in the gentle breeze, and daffodils trumpeted everlasting creation. Crickets chirped in unison, and butterflies flitted back and forth, resting on his shoulders and hovering over the wildflowers sparkling with fairy dust. Waterfalls from the rain he had created cascaded over rock-laden streams in a steady rhythm. The woodlands, which he had painted in forty or more hues of green, were his favorite place in this celestial world he inhabited.

Soon woodland sprites emerged from the hewn holes of the trees populating the glen and from the roots beneath them. Dryads of the trees with elongated, flowing arms and almond-shaped eyes; wood nymphs with skin of bark and red eyes; plant fairies with translucent faces resembling the flowers they tended; rock people and devas of the glen; and gnomes gathered. Dwarves climbed out from their underground abode and appeared at their cave entrance. All took their places in the stone circle.

The Green Man stood at the center stone and thanked them for heeding Gaia's call to join his legion on Earth. He expressed gratitude to the nature guardians for their dedication and readied them for their journey. He then raised his arm toward them. A beam of light issued from his hand, diffusing the area with a green mist. Orbs popped out of the misty cloud, spinning in rapid descent. Tiny drops of mist settled lightly on the energy form of the Green Man. Branches of leaves and vines grew over his head, and he was soon covered from head to foot with forest greenery. Hawthorn was woven into the crown of leaves on his head. In a booming voice, he directed the orbs to follow him. They swirled about him, spinning faster and faster into a vortex of brilliant emerald light. The vortex lifted off the ground, arched up into the sky, and then dived down in a steep plummet to Earth.

The Green Man and his legion materialized in the Earth plane on the summit of Mount Shasta. There they waited for Gaia. Soon an image of Gaia formed in the Green Man's mind. Robust scents of rich soil, ripe fruit, and perfumed flowers preceded her manifestation. She radiated a golden glow of love so absolute and pure that the Green Man thought he could not contain his joy. He loved his queen and would pursue any quest in her honor.

The Green Man bowed in reverence before her. Cloaked in a mantle of velvety green, its billowing folds undulating in the rhythmic beat of life, the beneficent matron motioned for him to stand. "You are steadfast in your service to me. For that I am grateful."

"There is no other cause more paramount in my heart than the salvation of the people of this planet," he replied.

"There is much suffering in this world. The hearts of humanity are heavy and weary of their tragedies and the discord they must daily endure," Gaia acknowledged. "Their suffering has cast a pall over the planet. A dense energy blankets the Earth, causing enmity to spread farther, creating despair and helplessness, suffocating all hope of a better place in which to live. We have tried with all our means to lift our world out of these dark doldrums. But the nature guardians dwelling on the planet and I have grown weak holding the elements of this planet in harmony and balance. Their light is fading.

"We will work together to restore peace and love in the hearts of mankind. Your granddaughter is pure of heart. Her heart will sing the intention of creating a peaceful world and of opening humanity's awareness to love—one heart at a time. Her purity of mind, with intention and dedication, will touch and change many, the societies of peoples, and the world. We are all connected to one another on some level. Together, with the same intention, through our connection we will effect change. We will co-create; dream a peaceful world into being. Take her and her tribe to the sacred well deep in the forest. Thereupon invoke the spirit of creation, an aspect embodied in the water spirit there, Melusina, to aid you in dreaming a peaceful world into being."

The Green Man took the nature guardians, his granddaughter of pure heart, and her tribe to the sacred well in the forest. There, they gathered.

"My beloved granddaughter, I am overcome with joy to see you again," the Green Man greeted his granddaughter. "Your heart is pure and holds unconditional love and peace. We ask you to sing the song of new beginnings, our song of co-creation. It will awaken the pure nature necessary to save the rest of humanity. Sing, now, my granddaughter."

The girl stepped before the sacred well with nobility and grace. She raised her arms and began to sing the co-creation song of her heart—pure, clear, and bright as the dawning sun. The vibration of the song emanated outward in concentric circles, touching all the assembly.

Awaken, loved ones,
Awaken, loved ones,
To the rising sun,
To the new day's light.
A new world dawns, and
We pave the way.
Join hearts in love,
Hands in peace,
As Earth is transformed.
A land of harmony and hope,
Acceptance and abundance,
Joyful and whole, where
All fears are vanquished,
All hatreds cease.
All are healed in a
World of never-ending
Promise and possibility.

They took each other's hands and in unison held the song, a common vision, in their hearts, and their dream of a new world came into being. The vibration of the song reverberated against the sides of the well and the water in the well began to ripple, awakening Melusina slumbering in its depths.

The Green Man summoned the spirit. “I invoke you, Melusina, spirit of the well, to come forth. Show us the world we are co-creating in this moment.”

A conch shell lay at the bottom of the well. The shell began to rotate in the gentle motion of the rippling water, slowly at first, then gaining speed, to create a whirlpool. As the water spun faster and faster, a water spirit with long, swirling sandy hair garbed in aquamarine frothy water twisted out of the shell and rose to the surface. Her sinuous arms, like seaweed, beckoned to the co-creators gathered around the well. The water spirit showed them the vision they were dreaming into being.

They saw the vibration of the co-creation song amplify throughout the globe. They saw men, women, and children rise up, one after the other, resonating with the vibration of the song and awakening to the light of love and peace like the petals of a flower opening to the morning sun. They too held the song in their hearts, until all inhabitants of Earth were pure of heart and their spirits were awakened.

Gaia and her nature guardians joined the assembly at the sacred well. Benevolent beings from the higher dimensions arrived to aid them in spreading love and healing around the globe. The assembly saw themselves rising in a ring around the planet, their hands extended toward it. Their palms emitted green healing light and the pink light of love. Earth was awash with this healing light and vibrating love.

They saw the Earth bathed in the radiance of compassion and forgiveness, wisdom and understanding, respect and acceptance. They saw harmony and balance restored to the planet. They saw the utopia they brought into existence, a utopia of peace and prosperity, health and happiness, community and cooperation. They saw the vision of their co-creation and were grateful.

Their intention set, now all they were to do was await the manifestation of the peaceful world they had envisioned. Confident that it would come, they were grateful in the knowing. Before the assembly dispersed Gaia conferred the title of *Keeper of Peace* upon the girl to show her deep gratitude. She raised her arms over the head of the girl. Golden droplets of light formed over the girl's head. They hovered there for a moment as Gaia spoke to her.

Pure of heart,
Heart divine,
Your light of love
Shines bright.
Bearer of peace,
Lead the way.
Peace, compassion,
Bring to light.

When she was finished, the droplets slowly descended onto the head of the girl, settling on her in a rhythmic beat. Gaia had planted seeds of her eternal love in the pure heart of the girl, who would sow these seeds into the hearts of humanity. The Green Man bowed in his profound reverence for his granddaughter and took his leave. He and his assembly of guardians ascended to their wooded glen in the spirit realm.

The girl and her tribe went back to their peaceful way of life. Everywhere she went, onto everyone she met, she shined her light, sowing Gaia's seeds of love. They in turn shined their light upon everyone they met, everywhere they went. Soon all the hearts of all the people in the world were lit with love and peace.

They worked together to maintain harmony and balance in the world. The peoples of the world came to respect each other by listening with empathy, imagining what it was like to be in one another's place. They soon found it easy to accept the differences in their beliefs and performed many loving acts of kindness. They settled old scores and negotiated peaceful settlements to disputed territories. They shared resources and supported one another, rendering aid when needed. No one was left destitute. In their hearts, trust replaced fear, unconditional acceptance replaced judgment, respect for all life replaced enmity, love replaced hatred, and happiness replaced suffering. All inhabitants of the planet lived in gratitude and joy.

And a peaceful world came into being.

CHAPTER *Seven*

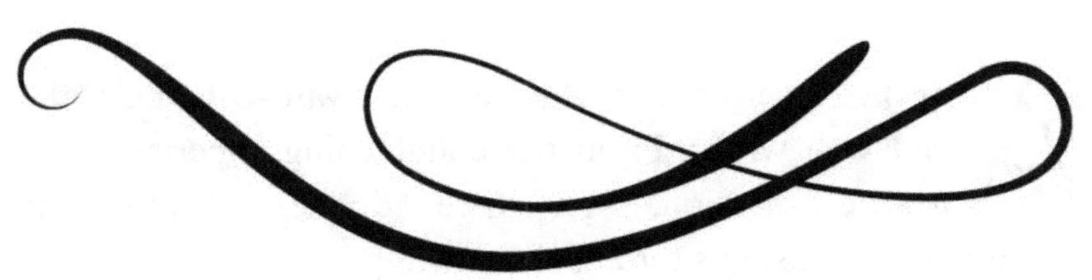

Are You My Soul Mate?

ANN E. AGUELI

Ann E. Agueli is a spiritual writer, award-winning author, and web writer. From her enlightening experiences and heartfelt passion, Ann shares divine inspiration and transformational insights through her writing.

Ann is the author of "When God Nods: Inspirational Tales of Divine Serendipity," a collection of stories where serendipity and divinity intertwine. This book offers inspiring stories of connection; some are astonishing while others are humorous, but all will leave you feeling moved and motivated. You will gain insights on how to uncover the lessons and discover the blessings ... *"When God Nods."*

"When God Nods: Inspirational Tales of Divine Serendipity" invites you to open up to the powerful and majestic love of your higher power. Page by page, this book will leave you amazed,

enlightened, and inspired.

You can check out more of Ann's inspirational writings, transformational books and services or contact her for life coaching in spiritual and relationship matters on her website: www.theinspiredlivingnetwork.com.

Ann's Other Books:

- *When God Nods: Inspirational Tales of Divine Serendipity*
- *Transformational Journaling for Mind, Body, Spirit*
- *Joy-Full Journaling for the Caregiver's Spirit: A Transformational Workbook*

(Both journal books are filled with inspirational quotes, transformative exercises, and powerful "I AM" affirmations.)

You can find these on www.theinspiredlivingnetwork.com or on Amazon.com.

Ann also owns:

Inspire Content: www.inspirecontent.com where she uses her creative talents and heart for helping others to handle writing projects from consulting to content creation. Content is the connection and she is the bridge; her writing makes a difference—one word at a time.

Inspire Caregivers: www.inspirecaregivers.com where caregivers, elder care, and spirituality meet.

Contact:

email: justwrite721@gmail.com

ACKNOWLEDGEMENT

To my three biggest blessings, my children Ralph, Julianna, and Annalesa, God has graced me abundantly with your presence. You are all beyond amazing.

In memory of my mom, who just passed away.

My gratitude to God, for the coincidences and serendipities,

For angels seen and unseen, and

To the life lessons that became life's blessings

DEDICATION

To all divine souls living in human beings

To God, for nodding at me

To my children: I am so blessed and so proud. Each of you desires to make a difference

To my parents for waiting on God's promise to have me

To my soul tribe: I honor and adore you; to Shanda Trofe, I'm grateful

To my lessons and the ability to turn them into blessings.

So be it (Amen).

Are You My Soul Mate? Relationships, Reflections, & Revelations

ANN E. AGUELI

Daddy's Little Girl

Shortly before my dad began the journey toward the end of his life, I began searching for something more—the elusive something more. When I became open to the possibility of spirituality, the first coincidence was discovering a transformational seminar. During that seminar, I was given a gift; the gift of healing with my dad. I discovered there were stories in my head about my father's love for me. I didn't find out until much later in life that he grew up in an orphanage. He had a hard life. I interpreted Dad's ways of viewing life, as speaking about me, my value, and my worth.

The Peaceful Ending: After completing the seminar, I went to the hospital to rewrite the story of our relationship, "Dad, you were the best dad to me you could have been." His response—"I hope so."

"Well, Dad, you don't have to hope; now you know." This was our last conversation; he lost the ability to speak. Two days later, he was gone. When he passed (even though it was the dead of winter, at night) there was pure light, joy, and, yes, the palpable presence of peace in the room. My search for something more turned into the possibility of peace; peace here on earth for me and eternal peace for him.

In forgiveness, there is release and in release, there is peace.

Twin Flame: What's in a Name?

As I went along my journey, coincidences and serendipities swirled around me like the tornado in the Wizard of Oz. Sometimes, I found myself in strange places wishing to go home again. I wanted to hold onto the old, familiar yet limiting, self-sabotaging beliefs about relationships. Letting go and recognizing I had the power within the whole time required a sort of bravery I was not yet ready to acknowledge. I had to first follow the yellow brick road, face my lions, tigers, and bears and meet the wicked witch—oh yes, I did! I was determined, however, to meet the wizard. So I began my journey.

I loved with all I had; trusted with all I had; gave it all away. And then, I began to do the work. I read, prayed, researched, talked, and dug deep to discover, or rather uncover, the multiple layers of my "self." Here are a few things I learned along my way. If I can help you gain a little glimmer of insight, it would make my heart sing.

Of course, I knew the term "soul mate." Who didn't? However, I had never heard the term "Twin Flame" until my soul-sister enlightened me. I was convinced this man was my "Twin Flame." I would think of him; my phone would vibrate, and it was him. I would feel his energy and there would be an email that wasn't there a moment ago. Just about everywhere I went, his name would show up (and he doesn't have a common name). I would feel his spirit so deeply like nothing I had ever known or could even begin to put into words.

One day, I brought my sick pup to the veterinarian's. They took him from me to care for him and I went over to the sink to wash my hands. Next to the sink was a doggie statue, and on his name tag was my friend's name with a cute slogan on it. I laughed, feeling the joy with all my heart.

When my dad was passing, I went to the hospital and asked if the priest had come to give him last rites; the answer was, of course, yes, and that the priest who gave my dad last rites had the same name as my friend.

He was truly my soul mate; not as the romance novel-type of soul mate, but "the one" who came here to teach me the lessons I refused to learn otherwise. It wasn't until I was willing to take responsibility for my life that my life truly became my own. I had the power to create my journey, to show up as I chose in the area of relationships, and I was fully going to use my newfound superpowers.

Unconditional Love: I choose to believe God was setting things up for someone to watch out for me and teach me about valuing and loving myself, as Dad began to leave this earthly realm. I needed to learn to love, honor, and value myself; this was my biggest life lesson. I learned my value and worth do not come from anyone else or anything else—not a parent, a lover, a friend, a degree or any number of accolades, not even an accumulation of finances. God loves me and I love me too.

Talk about unconditional love. God loved me so much he orchestrated someone appearing to make me cry, learn, sing, soar, sink, and dance all at the same time. I learned something else, and I want this for you too.

Empowered and Enlightened: Whenever I go into "wounded little girl" mode, I ask myself an important question, "What would powerful woman Ann do in this moment?" She would love herself exactly as she loves her own children, unconditionally, without thinking and without blinking; effortlessly and gracefully, with ease and flow. And as my life becomes transformed, it becomes transparent, and it becomes mine!

I stepped into the shoes of the woman I was meant to be when I allowed the little girl inside of me to take a nap until the next time she comes out to play. She teaches me about unconditional love more than anyone else I know. Without my soul mate, I wouldn't have learned to navigate these tricky waters. He challenged me and exasperated me. The more he threw my way, the more determined I became to catch it, recreate it, and mold it into something that would work for me. I grew and I transformed. I rode the wave and wound up somehow miraculously standing on my own two feet feeling more like my "self" than ever before. However, you can't ride the waves until you dive into the ocean. I remember the lessons and the blessings, and I wouldn't change a thing. I consider myself blessed to be able to say I met my soul mate here on earth.

The Peaceful Ending: It's no one's job to validate us. Ego strives to get the one person who doesn't quite love us the way we need to be loved, to love us better and more than anyone else. It's a missing piece of the childhood puzzle that may still be unresolved. Only difference is, we can resolve it on our own.

Let go of trying to "win" unavailable love and affection from a man in order to be validated. Create a new story of already being loved and adored in your own right just by being you. Allow the right man to gain your love and affection instead of working so hard to win it for yourself. Let go of winning; don't chase or try to win that emotion when it is unavailable.

Make a Wish on Love

At my favorite place in the world, The Vanderbilt Mansion, there's a wishing well. I threw a coin over my shoulder and made a delightful wish. I went to look for the coin, it was nowhere to be found. It wasn't on the floor or in the well; it landed right inside the pot hanging in the center of the wishing well. A year later, someone would come into my life and into my world at the exact moment my mom began her journey home to heaven a few short months ago.

Coincidence? I think not. God was gracious enough to send someone to help ease my sorrow in losing my mom. Not only was she my mom, but I was her caregiver and she lived with me. After many relationships that were not good for me, God honored my wish with this man. I took him to the wishing well and, yes, he kissed me there.

I was struck by fear and made every excuse in the book not to get close to him; I was anxious and afraid of a future upset that hadn't yet occurred. I was afraid of falling in love again and of getting hurt, one more time.

Only thing is, he went above and beyond to show me differently. Through this relationship came the awareness I gained about what was possible for me from a man. After many hurtful relationships, I didn't have the slightest idea a man could treat me with so much adoration and affection; the way he looked at me was genuine. I had never known this as a possibility. ***To him it was a given; to me it was a gift.***

The story doesn't end here though; there's a plot twist. He entered into our new relationship without having rectified his past. Combined with growing, strong feelings for me and seeing what was possible with a life partner such as me, his confusion grew. He's also relocating to North Carolina, and in this moment, it has ended. It was the shortest, sweetest, life lesson-learning relationship I'd ever had. Although it was filled with unfinished business from the past, it showed potential for a powerful partnership in the future.

The Peaceful Ending: I was incomplete. I didn't get to say all I wanted. Suddenly, this feeling of overwhelming peace came to me like never before; I heard my intuition clearly and audibly—"You will speak to him again." I made the call. I honored my feelings without making them right or wrong and without making him wrong. I spoke my truth with compassion, and it was beautiful, but most of all, it was peaceful.

Sad but true, each being is here to take this journey one step (or three) at a time. Sometimes we meet the right person at the absolutely wrong moment. Other times, our encounters with others are brief and powerful, yet fleeting.

They enter your life to shine a light on something and offer it to you as a gift; while we, on the other hand, unbeknownst to us, are a gift and contribution to them, as well. One more stepping stone on the journey toward healing and wholeness, we are a piece of their puzzle called life, as they are to us.

There are no wrong steps, no wrong turns, just an ever-forward, free-flowing series of events. Some stones in our pathways are smaller while others require giant leaps to travel across; each one, however, is just as significant as the other no matter how big or how small. The journey is a pathway, all of which is a whole; no step is inconsequential and no leap of faith too great.

Endings or Beginnings? Do I look at this as one more loss and another ending or do I view it as a new beginning? The choice is always ours and while some days are better—much better—than others, I can honestly say I've been through enough and know enough to say this time I'll work on waiting to see what unfolds. I don't do well in situations where I don't know what the ending is. (I love spoiler alerts!) Maybe I'll relocate too or maybe God has other plans for me; only He knows.

Funny thing, as I went for a walk on the boardwalk recently, bumping into a neighbor, he asked me now that my youngest has left the nest, why don't I downsize and maybe move to North Carolina?

Curious, intriguing, and amusing all rolled into one. I actually am traveling to North Carolina this fall. One thing is for sure, however, this time I'll just have to learn to sit back and wait—once again in my life—until next time,

When God Nods.

CHAPTER

A Gift from Thomas

TERRI WALLACE

Terri Wallace is an interspecies communicator specializing in Animal Communication, and a Holistic Healer. From a young age, she has been able to communicate with all species of beings, both living and passed. She has worked with a variety of domestic and wild animals, as well as plants, minerals, and many loving beings in spirit. It is her goal to raise awareness and advance interspecies relationships, on both personal and spiritual levels. Through her work, she guides people to deepen their connection with all species in an honoring manner, and is inspired to be a voice for the animals and our natural environment. She is passionate about sharing her knowledge of the Animal, Plant, Insect and Mineral Kingdoms.

Terri has studied a variety of holistic modalities to assist animals and people through the healing process in all stages of life. Some of the modalities include Reiki, Crystal Healing, Aromatherapy and Herbal Remedies. Terri practices Mayan-based Shamanism, and has achieved certifications as a Reiki Master/Teacher, Mind,

Body and Spirit Practitioner, Animal Psychology and Ordained Minister. She attended St. Petersburg College in Florida for International Business and has run several of her own businesses.

Terri offers communication consultations, natural healing services, grief counseling and a variety of workshops and training in Animal Communication, Plant Communication, Animal Reiki training, and other Holistic Healing Modalities.

In addition to working as a communicator, Terri is the Founder and Director of the Earth Healing Foundation. It is a non-profit organization that brings healing to the cycle of abuse through education by providing community programs that promote increased awareness, empathy, compassion and mutual understanding between humans, animals and the natural world.

Connect with Terri

Email: animalhealer.tw@gmail.com

Websites

www.earthhealing4animals.com.

www.earthhealingfoundation.com.

Social Media

www.facebook.com/terri.wallace.10

www.facebook.com/earthhealingforanimalsfoundation/

www.facebook.com/Earth-Healing-for-Animals-526557097366111/

www.twitter.com/twanimalhealer

ACKNOWLEDGEMENT

I would like to express my gratitude with much love and many thanks to Thomas the cat; my daughter, Melissa Kitzmiller; and my friends Jessica Grosse, Kelli Demski, Tara Jack, Michael Leclerc and Shanda Trofe for supporting me in my journey in writing this chapter.

DEDICATION

This chapter is dedicated to all of the loving beings who share their compassion with others.

A Gift from Thomas

TERRI WALLACE

Thomas came into my life through a friend one day in April 2016. I had been staying with friends during a transitional period in my life. I was healing from three years of what seemed like one continuous loss after another. I had just returned home from work when my friend Jessica met me in the driveway. She started telling me about what had happened on a walk she had taken with her boyfriend Mike earlier in the neighborhood. It had started to get warm as they were walking so Mike suggested they go down another street that was lined with trees to walk in the shade. As they continued, an animal came into view, lying across the sidewalk. As they came closer, they realized that it was an orange tiger-striped cat and wondered why it wasn't moving. Most cats move when being approached. This one did not, almost as if it wanted to block their path.

They stopped to see what wrong with the cat. As they began talking to it, he got up and rubbed their hands and legs like cats do when saying hello. Jessica noticed that the cat had some trouble breathing and was walking stiffly. He was wheezing and his breathing was labored. Taking a closer look, Mike saw that there were multiple puncture wounds around the cat's neck, head and back. Fur was also missing in several spots. It was obvious that there had been some sort of fight and this cat survived but wasn't doing well. Jessica and Mike checked with the nearby houses to see if anyone claimed ownership, but no one did. One woman did say that she had seen him in the area for the last week and a half. She had been caring for the cat by putting out food for it, while her neighbor was providing fresh water every day. The woman didn't have the money to take the cat to the vet so she was doing what she could. She told Mike that the cat was always in the street, almost as if he wanted someone to run him over and put him out of his misery.

As Jessica was telling me what had happened, my thoughts kept asking, what is wrong with everyone? It broke my heart; I felt that no one had the same compassion for this cat that I had. Then it became clear to me. He had the same compassion for me that I had for him. He came to remind me that even though we are the same on the inside, we each have our own levels of compassion. After listening to the story, I asked Jessica if she thought the cat was ready to die, and she said she felt that he was and that he didn't want to continue living as he had been.

A few minutes later, we went inside, grabbed a towel to wrap him in and decided to ask the cat if he wanted to come with us to see the vet. The two of us drove the seven or eight blocks to where she had encountered the cat. He was still on the sidewalk right where she had left him close to four hours earlier, almost like he knew we were coming and didn't want to miss us. I pulled up as close to the sidewalk as I could; he didn't move at all. As we sat on the sidewalk discussing our options, he came up to Jessica then to me, letting us check his wounds. He allowed us to pick him up and thoroughly inspect him. He had a damaged tail and two sore legs, the right front being the worst. He did not appreciate my touching that one at all, but he let me. It was surprising that not once did he try to bite or scratch either one of us, as if he knew we were there to help him.

I asked what he wanted to do—"go home" or stay. Either way we would take him to the vet and get an opinion. He then climbed into my lap and said he would go see the doc. I explained that we would take him with us and he would have to stay for a day or so at the house until the vet could see him. I also let him know that we had multiple animals living with us. He didn't care. He was willing to go. I wrapped the blanket around him and Jessica drove us back to the house. He was very content just sitting on my lap. We kept him separated so he could rest and not be disturbed by the other very curious animals. He let us clean his wounds and take a closer look at his body. He had trouble eating because he couldn't breathe easily. After he was clean and had a full belly, we took turns holding and comforting him.

After some time, he revealed the name Thomas to me. He then went on to say his full name was Thomas Aquinas. The name sounded familiar but we couldn't place it, so Jessica looked it up and we found it fit him perfectly and explained why he came when he did. According to the Catholic Church, Thomas Aquinas was a Saint and a philosopher. He had struggled much of his life and wanted to become a Dominican priest but his family did not agree. They kidnapped and held Thomas hostage for a few years to prevent him from joining the order. Finally the family gave in to his wishes. He felt it was his purpose and had never given up trying to leave his family.

Thomas Aquinas had several writings throughout his lifetime, but his greatest work is considered to be the *Summa*, which was his opinion on God and love. I felt the message that Thomas the cat was sharing with me was that we are all spiritual beings and love is the fundamental relationship of all who exist in this world. It is what connects us to each other. Love is available for every being and all beings are equal. As a psychic medium with a specialty in inter-species communication, I am able to speak with all beings, including animals. I interpret their thoughts, feelings and language, translating them into a language that humans can understand.

When asked what had happened to him, Thomas the cat said that he had been hurt by some kids. They kicked him a couple of times, swung him around by his tail and chased him. He eventually became disoriented and was lost at some point. The people he had been staying with didn't want him anymore so they put him out and stopped taking care of him. He was giving up on life. He wanted to die, to go back to the place that's called home or heaven by most beings. He said it's beautiful, with no trouble, pain or worries. All are equal there and filled with love. So he made arrangements with another animal to be merciful and kill him. The attack was stopped by someone in the neighborhood. Soon after the attack, he was told to stay on that street where he would be given food and water until he met us.

Little did I know that he would be waiting for me. I had been feeling very much like him. Life had been extremely hard on me for the last three years. Many beloved beings that were close to me had made their transition unexpectedly. The first two were my dog Sierra and my cat Odie on my move from Maryland to Arizona in January 2013. Shortly after I arrived in Arizona, my dog Leiza made her transition in May. In September, Sam, a man who had become like a father-in-law to me, and a week later, my Uncle Joe, passed away. In November it was my cat Bonnie Girl, December was my cat Tim, then my dog Romeo in June of 2014, and DC my girl kitty in August. December brought the loss of my Aunt Misty, who was married to Uncle Joe and was like a big sister or second mother to me. My younger sister Patti transitioned in March of 2015 and my dad followed in August. It seemed everyone close to me was going home. It finally became too much after a breakup in November and moving yet again in February 2016. I felt just like Thomas; tired, alone, unloved and beaten. All of us as individuals want to be loved by others unconditionally. To have such love tells us we belong, we are important, we are wanted and we have a purpose. We release our fears when we feel compassion, empathy and kindness; all are fundamental parts of love.

Over the next few weeks Thomas would improve slightly and then decline. He was taking breathing treatments, fluids and a few different medicines. He enjoyed being around each of us, including the other cats. He slept a lot as many people supported him physically, emotionally and spiritually. If he chose to stay, it was going to be a struggle because of the condition his body was in, but there were lots of people willing to help him. Thomas had many tests done to try to determine what was happening in his body. The vet found that he had multiple puncture wounds, and swollen tissue in the nose that was complicating his breathing; he had been shot with a bb, had inflammation in his abdomen and a broken tail.

Thomas came to us to feel loved, wanted and that he mattered, at least for a little while. He also was here to remind us to have love, kindness and compassion not only for others but for ourselves as well. We all come from the same place no matter what form we take here on earth. What we do to others we do to ourselves. All Thomas and I wanted in those weeks was to feel loved and to know that we matter, we are important to others. Everyone at some point in their life has similar feelings. So if every moment that we encounter another being, we were to show compassion, kindness, love, mercy and understanding, the world would be, in my experience, a much better place.

People are missing the piece that fills them up, and often look for something to replace it. That missing piece is love. Usually material things are what people substitute for filling up the emptiness. People become disconnected from their spirit. Fear, anger, and frustration then come in and take over. What do you choose? Love or Fear? Love is what I choose and Thomas was a great reminder for me when I felt lost. Sometimes all of us could use a reminder—to remember where you come from, a place of love. Thomas died a few weeks after he arrived. He made a huge impact on all of us. Thomas received what he came here for: to be loved, seen, heard and cared for.

I had reached the point where I no longer wanted to talk to people and translate the language of the animals for them. Thomas came to remind me that I am loved and even though I said no to more interpreting, I still felt compassion and love for others like he did, even when we were down and out. Love is what keeps us all connected. The disconnection comes with fear and negativity. Thomas knew that by reconnecting me with love and compassion for another that I would pick myself up and continue on with my purpose. To help the animals, be their voice to the humans, to show love, kindness and mercy to all beings. To remind those who are in a similar place, that they are loved. To help them reconnect their spirit with the whole. I translate the languages of other beings to humans to reconnect all of us back to love. I do this for the love of the animals just as they do it for the love of all.

Take Joy

The gloom of the world is but a shadow,
    behind it, yet within reach, is joy.
There is radiance and glory in the darkness
    could we but see and to see we have only to look.
I beseech you to look.

Life is so generous a giver, but we, judging its gift by their covering,
    cast them away as ugly or heavy or hard.
Remove the covering and you will find beneath it a living splendor,
    woven of love by wisdom, with power.

Welcome it, grasp it,
    and you touch the angel's hand that brings it to you.
Everything we call a trial, a sorrow, or a duty,
    the angel's hand is there, the gift is there
    and the wonder of an overshadowing presence.
Our joys too, be not content with them as joys.
They too conceal diviner gifts.

And so at this time I greet you,
    not quite as the world sends greetings
But with profound esteem
    and with the prayer that for you, now and forever,
    The day breaks and the shadows flee away.

~Fra Giovanni- 1513

CHAPTER

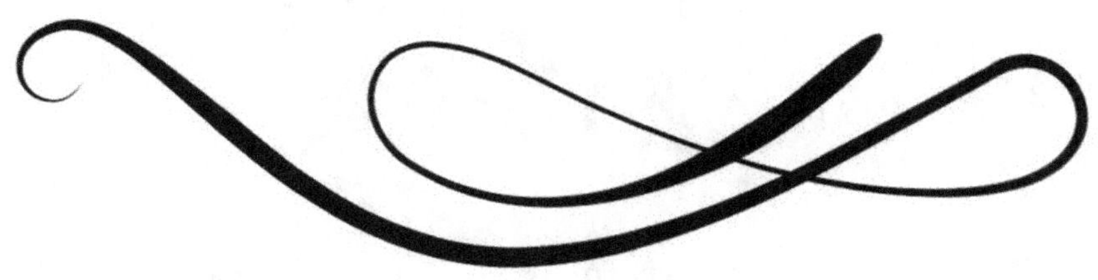

Peace is an Inside Job

FAITH FRIENDT-KLINGSPORN

Faith Friendt-Klingsporn is an inspired teacher, healer, neuro-linguistic life coach, hypnotherapist, reiki healer, "access consciousness bars facilitator" and medium. She is active in church, and has served on church council. Faith and her partner Cindy have founded the "Women in Transition" group to bring together women of all ages to share friendship, wisdom and healing. Faith is currently attending The Lay School of Ministry of the Northwest Synod of Wisconsin, which assists lay people in finding a deeper Christian identity and fosters participation in church mission.

Faith has risen from tremendous adversity by utilizing many healing modalities. Her quest to heal and to break cycles of unhealthy abuse patterns spans fifty years. She is both a fighter and a survivor! Finding her purpose came through marriage at 16, having four loving children, finding out she is gay at 34, getting a divorce and being at death's door in 2009, all while shuffling through the pain of sexual, emotional, and physical abuse. The power of God's Spirit in her heart has led Faith to both traditional and non-traditional therapy and healing modalities. Faith has a heart for helping people learn to accept themselves unconditionally and teaching them how to heal!

Connect with Faith

Email: info@faithfriendtklingsporn.com

Website: www.FaithFriendtKlingsporn.com

Social Media

www.facebook.com/ faithfriendt-klingsporn

www.facebook/angelsoverthewater

www.twitter.com/FKlingsporn

ACKNOWLEDGEMENT

To my partner Cindy, your unconditional love brings me peace and inspiration. Many thanks to my beautiful family and friends for their patience, and my Bethany sisters for their never-ending encouragement. To those who taught me trust, I could not have completed this without your generous time and expertise: my sister Ellen and her husband Frank, my niece Jolene, and my sister-at-heart Lorraine Smyth. And of course my publisher and teacher, Shanda Trofe!

DEDICATION

This chapter is dedicated to my beautiful children Alan Jr, Kristine, Brian and Joshua. I am blessed beyond measure to be your mother. Breaking down the abuse cycles of my past has taken us all through much unintended pain. Your unconditional love is irreplaceable. I love you!

Peace is an Inside Job

Ready, Open-Minded and Willing To Heal!

FAITH FRIENDT-KLINGSPORN

Each of us is born a sweet and innocent little soul and a defenseless spirit longing to be snuggled and held. The design for our lives yet to be unveiled! Our greatest feat in this lifetime is to, in harmony, combine the essence of our higher self and our human self. In doing so, we decode the invisible inner consciousness, revealing the path etched upon the core of our soul, in the heart.

Never fear: The light of God is in the heart of all humans. Regardless of the deserted island a heart can become, the heart is always open to choosing love and recreating its new landscape.

Encountering events in life that are outside of our control can leave us feeling hopeless, as if an organism has invaded our lives, leaving us with a life sentence of helplessness. Experiences that may seem impossible can be changed to reveal the unlimited hope of the spirit. My Spirit had the power at such a time to shift me out of my body, saving me from what may have had the capacity to steal an entire lifetime of innocence. More on this later!

This infinite intelligence is connected to the source—whoever your higher power is—and there is always the opportunity to tap into knowing what you need to heal.

The Healing Begins

As I grew, my path was temporarily diverted through choices dictated by my past; this attracted more lessons of physical, mental and emotional abuse. Human pain became a distraction, drawing me away from my spiritual path. My God Positioning System (GPS) was out of reach and my authentic-self was at stake.

We can see ourselves as victims of traumatic circumstances, or seek hope in the shelter of knowing that when we call on God he will reveal his miracles.

Seeking my true emotions and the divine blueprint for my soul allowed me to connect to his light and opened my path to redemption.

I had always innately known that life held more than I could see; I recognized an awareness of this hope and peace within. Getting out of my own way to allow my inner spirit to be directed would mean tapping into the unseen force that speaks through each of our hearts.

Lessons

Abuse forced me to have skills I would not have otherwise had, forcing me to sort through my values. These choices can bring us face-to-face with love. The fact that we can choose love at any moment was revealed to me through a moment of clarity that seemed to be late, but was perfect in God's divine timing. The wakeup call that healed me in the depths of my heart came when I was faced with the knowledge that my mother had Alzheimer's disease and would need us to care for her. Until this time I had blamed her for the years of abuse that muted the conversation between my spirit and my soul and left me feeling lost; but in a pure moment of awareness, my direction shifted and a lifetime of heartache was healed in the matter of a second. I could remain a victim and believe that my experiences had irretrievably ruined my life, or I could acknowledge that I had a choice. My direction depended on what I chose to embrace. Was I going to be a victim or a victor?

Finding Courage

Hearing this bible verse allowed me to believe there was good to come!

Romans 8:28: "And we know that in all things God works for the good of those who love him, who have been called according to his purpose." (NIV)

Whatever your faith, know this; everything, including evil, can be used for good. I embraced this verse and held on for dear life.

When we trust God he leads us in extraordinary ways. While sitting in the office of a shiatsu healer I was stunned to hear my voice speak this sentence: "I don't know what it is you've got but I want it!" And as if pre-orchestrated and without another word, the woman handed me a file and said, "I think I know what you are talking about." There are no coincidences, for regardless of the number of difficult circumstances that had occurred, God had a plan for my life and he acted through this woman. I could have questioned what happened to me but I trusted God and believed in his word. I waited curiously to see how the plan would unfold in his time. Soon I was told our company was closing, which set the stage for a full-ride to the school revealed in that file. Receiving a certification in Neuro-Linguistic life coaching at the Meta Institute in Minneapolis, Minnesota was designed to save my life.

There, I began the journey of healing the pain that I had

allowed to keep me locked in the past. I chose not to bury what happened to me, even if no one else could confirm it. It hurt to the core, and the internal dialogue was deafening and painful. But in this silence, if I listened, the Source could speak to me and redirect my path and HE did.

One of the many truths the course work taught me was that experiences before the age of seven are called the imprint years in neuro-linguistics. An age span with no mental filters, this is a time when everything goes straight to the unconscious mind and so memories formed then are generally out of conscious awareness. The internal pain I experienced had seemed to come from an invisible source. As I developed I knew something was wrong and my lack of memories caused me to question my sanity. At five years of age I was about to experience what I am sure could have unraveled my peace for the rest of my life; instead, an out-of-body experience protected me. Instead of being in my body experiencing the degrading act, I was watching what was happening to me from a corner of the room in mid-air. It seems as if I remembered seeing it happen but had no cellular memory/feelings related to the event, which was very confusing.

The circumstances of my childhood left me feeling lost, alone and angry with God for their impact I was experiencing. I had been through more challenges than any human being should endure. My body was suffering adrenal damage and in 2009 I was at death's door. My hobby farm was in foreclosure and the animals there had been the reason I got out of bed, my relationship had ended, and I could barely function. But God's saving grace had sent me to school at the Meta Institute. Through that training I knew that what I believed was going to make or break me, body, mind and spirit. It was time for what seemed an impossible healing to begin.

I called on my higher power (for me that is God) to reveal the spiritual tools I needed, and I began the journey back to my heart by asking the Angels to help me. And to my surprise he answered by sending them! I glanced through the bay window overlooking the lake in front of my home and saw nine gleaming pillars of illuminated, glittering gold gracing my sight. I will never forget November 27th, 2013. I felt the Angels brought the encouragement of his promise and embodied the complete peace of healing that I had been asking for.

Attracting Help

We are created with free will so neither God nor the Angels can intervene without our request. On the website healyourlife.com, Doreen Virtue, The founder of Angel Therapy, states that upon asking God and the Angels why we can't just talk to God, she got this answer: *"When people are afraid and most in need of heaven-sent help, their vibrations are too low to hear and feel the pure love of God. The angels, who are closer to Earth, are easier to hear and feel when someone is fearful or stressed. They can lift the person's vibrations and help him or her to be unafraid and at peace and return to a clear connection with God."*

The fact that you are reading this book is not a coincidence. It is likely there was a series of events linked together by your higher power to help you. But you, my friend, have the free will to decide where your life will go. Your higher power is waiting for you to ask for help! I believe each of us carries God's image within our hearts. I urge you to embrace the hope of God and embrace the power within *you* to allow change and healing to happen in your life.

I wish for you to feel what I feel about the messages we get every day from our loving God. If you have a fear of being whom your Higher Power made you to be, or if you feel less capable than those around you, you are not alone. I was also afraid! But once I began to embrace my inner calling and realized that each of us is called to love as He does, everything changed. It is *your* journey and *your* internal calling that will change your world. You have come into this world given a voice and a choice to make a difference for yourself and others. I pray that you will find those that inspire you to build your courage as you move forward.

The Peace of Understanding

Bringing ourselves into alignment with peace is an "inside job." I encourage you to seek within the internal discord that affects you. Instead of wasting time beating yourself up over your internal dialogue, ask God to guide you and to provide you with the person or the knowledge you need to move forward to internal peace. Direct yourself to the internal—the spiritual—to tune into the infinite knowledge that does not come from human understanding. Seek and embrace the spiritual tools He provides. As we walk through this world there are many distractions limiting our reality. Once we have chosen to sit quietly and accept ourselves, our minds and hearts can be opened to receiving new possibilities.

Peace did not always come easy for me, and others did not always understand my actions. I had always felt such deep love for others that I could not judge them, even when their own pain was visited upon me in cruel ways. And, when I did not retaliate, I was seen by those close to me as weak. But all I could think was what Jesus said in part of Luke 23:34

> *Then said Jesus, Father, forgive them; for they know not what they do... (KJV)*

It was through spiritual guidance and understanding that I could see the future and know the consequences of my actions as well as theirs. They believed their intentions were good and called their behavior "tough love," but what I sensed was hatred. Seeking peace, I settled my heart knowing that people do the best they can with what they know at the time. Education comes daily in many forms and every day we are changed by our experiences.

My Life Was Changed

Many extraordinary occurrences are documented in scripture—that happened to humans walking this earth—yet we do not accept that it is within our being that Jesus lives.

God put His breath in our lungs and etched in each heart the ability to walk perfectly in His ways. He put the right people around us, to teach us and to love us, but in order to live fully, abundantly, healed, and liberated, each of us must trust Him with our hearts.

In the Sermon on the Mount, Matthew 7:7-8 Jesus says, "Ask and it will be given to you; seek and you will find; knock and the door will be opened to you. For everyone who asks receives; he who seeks finds; and to him who knocks, the door will be opened." (NIV)

"By our faith in Christ, we gain access to all
of God's treasures—joy,
peace and eternal life."
~Max Lucado
(Inspirational Study Bible)

CHAPTER

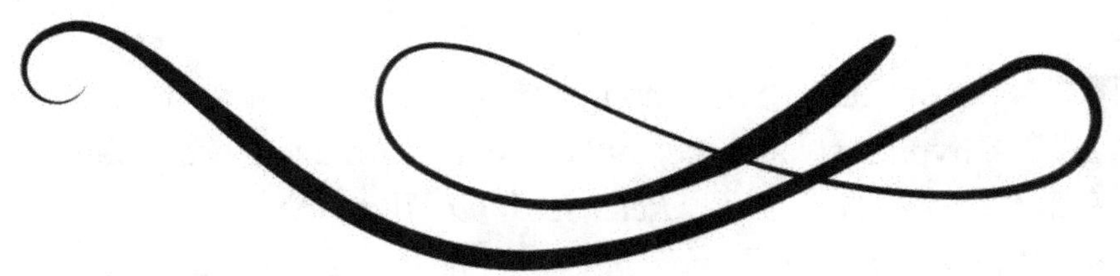

Life Continued

DARCY RENEE SIMONSON

Darcy Renee Simonson is an artist, personal growth guide, hypnotist and the author of the Amazon best-seller *To Love Your Life; Release What Was, Embrace What Is, and Become Wildly Wonderful You* and the accompanying *Life-Workbook.* Her creative and straight-forward personal growth work has guided thousands of people to explore their mental, emotional, physical and spiritual make-up, empowering them to live consciously, compassionately, and authentically. Darcy's books, workshops and over 25 hypnotic meditation audios for adults and children are available through her website. She is also the creator of EssenceSketch contemporary soul drawings, and in 2017 will debut WearOnPurpose.com in support of charities.

CONTACT

For information about Darcy's books, audios, and personal EssenceSketch soul drawings visit www.insightswithdarcy.com, and to shop with purpose at www.WearOnPurpose.com. Contact Darcy at darcy@insightswithdarcy.com

DEDICATION

Dedicated to Harriet Basset Price, William Hoff, and John Klassen. You continue to inspire and enrich my life. I look forward to seeing you again on the other side, if not before. - Darcy

Life Continued

DARCY R. SIMONSON

I am no lemming, much to the chagrin of authorities in the strict parochial school I endured for nine years. Rather, I am the sort of person who has to experience something to believe it, so when my teachers would tell me that God would punish me for doing something with which He or they didn't approve, that I would pay a high price unless I dropped a generous portion of my allowance in the offering plate every Sunday, or that my too-short skirt would raise the good Lord's eyebrow, I tested their convictions with fearless abandon. Most often, the truth was far less frightening than the one they wanted me to believe.

One well-intentioned message I'd hear from teachers and church elders after the death of someone I loved troubled me more than the others because I thought I might not be able to dispel it, at least not before it was too late. They would offer comfort by reassuring me that I would see my loved ones in heaven one day. They'd go on to say that those who have lived according to the rules of our religion will be waiting at the pearly gates to greet me, while those who didn't, well, they'd burn in hell – and of course the deceased was one of the former. I was never quite sure that was true. Grandma Virginia had a mean streak longer than the gravel road that lead to her farm, and Grandpa William smoked like a chimney – less than honorable traits, I'd been taught. Confused and concerned, I spent many years uneasy about what lies beyond the grave.

I eventually managed to find my way through the heaven and hell of my early years to a place of spiritual balance and peace in my conviction that a kind and loving higher power does exist. Still, like a faint scar from an old wound, residue from nine years of fire and brimstone conditioning lingered, particularly surrounding the mystery of life after death. I chose not to explore this mystery lest it lead me to discover that there *is* a hell, or even more frightening, there's nothing at all. Until a time when deep sadness and loss overcame my fear of knowing, that is.

Harriet's Caterpillar

I met Aunt Harriet in my twenties, three years before I married her nephew. We became fast friends. I appreciated her grit and guts, cultivated in spite of a silver spoon upbringing. She was good-humored, somewhat neurotic, and drank a bit too much. Her flawed-but-fearless attitude was not always popular with others, but I found it endearing. Harriet was one of the few women I knew who'd example what it is to live unapologetically, with determination, perseverance and strength. It was something I needed to witness to step more fully into my own feminine power.

Harriet relied on guts and grit to make it through her last year with as much grace as pancreatic cancer would allow. At her funeral I was too heartbroken to approach her urn. How was it possible such a big personality fit in such a small container? Following her fearless example, I put cowardliness aside and asked Harriet to send me a clear sign that she was happy and safe on the other side of life as we knew it.

After the funeral, people gathered to do something Harriet and I often stole away to do - sip wine over a visit on my wooded patio. My son pointed out a bug crawling on the chair near my fingertips. It was the insect I twenty years earlier had named Harriet's Caterpillar. Harriet would fight off the onslaught of what I have come to learn are army worms to keep them from devouring her trees. Her warrior-like effort to slay armies of worms before they could do too much damage made me giggle. Typically, the worms would arrive by the thousands, but that summer, in my tree-filled river lot, I saw only the one. Harriet answered my plea for reassurance that she was present, happy and safe through the very thing she knew I'd attribute to her – Harriet's Caterpillar.

Harriet's message made it clear to me that death is nothing more than a transmutation, and life continues with or without a physical body. Since Harriet's sign, my doubts and fears about life after death have subsided, and I've continued to witness the presence of deceased loved ones.

Grandpa's Cherry Lifesavers

Grandpa William was quiet, kind and earnest, and even though he had nearly 30 grandchildren, I always felt special when I was around him. Forty years after his death, I can't eat horseradish without hearing him laugh, board a fishing boat without seeing his hands, or pass by the old hospital in my hometown without remembering.

Grandpa was a carpenter who worked with asbestos before anyone knew asbestos kills. He was also a smoker. The toxic duo wreaked havoc on his heart and lungs. The last three months of his life were in a hospital bed, where my mother and I would visit him daily.

On the way to the hospital, mom and I would routinely stop at Kentucky Fried Chicken to pick up Grandpa's favorite meal. He'd eat what little of it he could, often just the tender nugget tucked against the thigh bone, and one or the other of us would finish. After his meal, Grandpa would give me a quarter and send me to the vending machine to buy him cherry Lifesavers. It was an errand I looked forward to, in part because he'd peel the first candy off the roll for me, but more so, I knew this treat was one of the few pleasures he had remaining and I could deliver it. In Grandpa's last few weeks of life, mom and I would drive by Kentucky Fried

Chicken; cherry Lifesavers were all he could stomach. I was thirteen years old when he died, but the sense of unconditional love and security I felt in his company, perhaps the only man I felt truly cherished by in my youth, never diminished.

Thirty-two years after Grandpa's death my eldest son graduated from high school. He was preparing to leave the state for college in Montana. The first of my three sons to fly from the nest I carefully constructed to keep my boys safe from imagined predators and parasites, I waffled between excitement for him and insecurity in my own changing role as his mother. Had I properly prepared him for life on his own? Had I cuddled and loved him enough to help him remember his worth when something or someone challenged it? I opened the door to his bedroom while he was packing for the sixteen-hour drive to his new home in Missoula when I was struck by an overwhelming smell of cherry. I asked him what the scent was coming from. He looked at me, bewildered. He couldn't smell cherries. Incredulous, we rolled eyes at each other, and I left the room.

I walked downstairs to the computer where another son was playing a game. I peeked over his shoulder with interest, and again the smell of cherry took me aback. "What is this?" I asked. Suddenly, I knew. It was the unmistakably strong, sweet scent of cherry Lifesaver. Grandpa had come to reassure me, as he did in my childhood, that all would be well. Grandpa presented, as Harriet had, when needed and in a manner I would clearly identify with him.

John's Gift

My youngest son flew from the nest the summer of 2016. As I contemplated the next phase of my life, I imagined a quaint, quiet home within which to create art, meditate, and re-discover myself outside of full-time motherhood. Where this place was, I didn't know. I considered a move to Colorado, an island on the pacific, or perhaps on a lake in already familiar Minnesota. Just as I was beginning to fret about not knowing my next move, a new friend mentioned a rustic cabin and four wooded acres on a quiet environmental lake near hers that would soon be for sale. It piqued my interest.

The cabin belonged to her father's friend, John, a wise, earnest, courageous man, with an intelligent sense of humor and a rebellious streak one might expect from a 71 year-old Minnesota born German Mennonite turned horse-breaking cowboy, canoe artist, multi-instrument musician and revered music teacher, re-rooted on a ranch in the mountains of western Montana. John spoke softly, wit danced on the end of his tongue, and gentleman that he was, he wasn't shy about expressing his opinions. A few minutes into our first phone conversation, John threw out a mildly provocative comment about presidential candidate Donald Trump, I'm certain to test my suitability as his cabin's suitor. I passed his playful inspection, and John told me where to find a hidden key to the cabin and outbuilding. I spent the weekend there, and on my 54th birthday asked John to sell me the place I'd already coined "Wildflower."

The following week, John was in Minnesota showing me around the property. We spent a long day together learning of each other's German heritage, strict religious upbringings, and how those things had influenced us. He told me stories about Victor, the good and wise man who had the cabin built forty years earlier. Victor was a German-Russian born Hutterite and history professor at my and John's alma mater. The divine coincidence was not lost on me - that the three of us were influenced by fundamental religions and German-Russian heritage; had in some capacity spent time at the same University; were teachers, practicing artists, musicians and/or authors; and now, shared keepers of, as John called it, the "artful" cabin and four wooded acres of pristine Minnesota lake land.

Victor wrote John about twenty years ago stating that if ever he sold the cabin it would be to him, his trusted friend. Victor unexpectedly died days after the letter was sent, and his widow sold the cabin to John. Twenty years later he passed the keys to me. On John's second trip to the cabin to close the sale, he gave me a few treasured gifts - a water-damaged Finnish missionary's bible he decades earlier had plucked from the trash while teaching at the White Earth Reservation in Minnesota. The gift made me cry. He thought it might as we shared reverence for indigenous people. The bible was a piece of history that brought some sadness and regret, a reminder of the subjection of Native Americans to western influence. He gave me a few pieces of furniture he'd built, a painting that leaves me curious, and a bird house he'd made for me even before we'd met. But moreover, John gave me his trust and friendship.

Ten days after I closed on the cabin, John called, excited to tell me that "my money" bought him a new horse. I was relieved to hear that this one was broke and ready to ride, as the last horse this seventy-one year old cowboy broke a summer ago caused a lingering concussion. I reminded John that I expect him and his wife to visit the cabin for a spell each summer. He said he'd bring his chainsaw when they came. I left that phone call filled with gratitude, appreciating how destiny brought this man and his artful cabin into my life. I don't know if it was John's resemblance to Grandpa William that kindled our familiarity, or because he was a kindred spirit, an old friend from lives gone by, but I do know that he and Wildflower were a blessing, Earth angels, really, in my newly forming future.

The evening of August 3, 2016, I went to Wildflower alone. I sat on the porch in the Adirondack chairs John built, watching summer raindrops dance on the water. While trying to recall the names of the many trees he'd pointed out to me I noticed a woodpile from a tree he downed and stacked so carefully before he left. In appreciation and awe, I watched the sun set and the moon rise. Tired, I moved into the cabin. I began to feel uneasy, as if I was being watched. I called a friend who soothed my fears and I drifted into a deep sleep. Three days later, just two weeks after John handed the cabin keys to me, I received a call - John died in an accident on August 3rd. In disbelief, I struggled to make sense of why this soul friend had come and gone so quickly. Through tears, I realized that the night I sensed I wasn't alone was the day John died. It was his presence I felt in the cabin. Just as Harriet and Grandpa William are still with me, I know in my heart John still watches over his beloved Minnesota cabin.

I regret that I will not get to know John better, but I take comfort in imagining him and Victor speaking German while paddling one of John's artfully crafted canoes in a heavenly little lake beyond the veil. I hope John continues to visit. Victor's welcome, too. After all, there's work to be done, stories to be told, and the spirit of love to be shared at the little haven in the woods, which destiny delivered to me with ease and grace, or as John said, "it was fortuitous that we met and the cabin go to you."

Harriet, Grandpa William and John helped me clear the last hurdle of religious dogma that didn't align with my belief in a loving God - one who'd invite our eternal souls home no matter how flawed we appear. Finally, before I had to die to discover the truth for myself, I was able to overcome trepidation around death. Each in their own way, my loved one's have shown me that death is not an ending, or even necessarily a good-bye. It is merely life continued.

CHAPTER Eleven

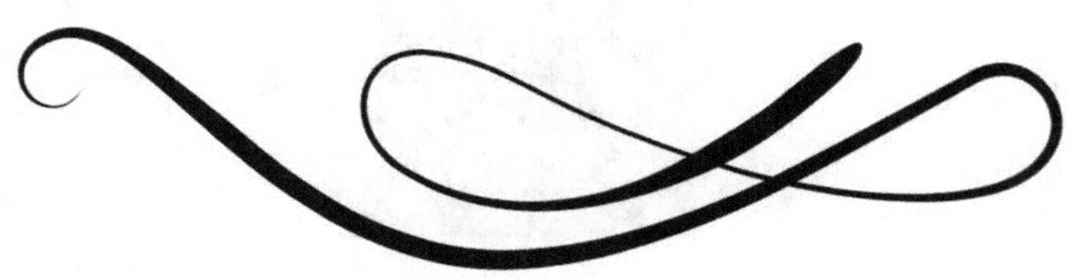

The Cyclical Wave of Soul

JANELLE FLETCHER

Janelle Fletcher's true calling is the honouring and empowerment of women, and she is a guiding light that helps women discover joy in the sacred, simplicity and the soul.

Intuitive, and holding onto a vision for what is possible, Janelle guides women to "find home" within themselves and their bodies, and teaches them how to step into their magnificence as a woman, mother and lover. Janelle's true gift is to help women find hope within their doubt, peace within their womanly struggles, and courage to honour the voice within.

A writer, speaker, wise-woman mentor and mother-heart, her global vision is to be ambassador of a cause empowering women and girls, and to continue travelling the world living simply, loving well and showing people the way to find their own light.

Dancing in Her Own Full Moonlight is her first book. Her poetry features in ***The Light Within: A Collection of Peace and Prose*** and she is a co-author of ***The Peace Makers*: *Restoring Love in the World through Stories of Compassion and Wisdom.***

Email: janelle@janellefletcher.com

Website: www.janellefletcher.com

SomeBODY Beautiful Community:

www.facebook.com/SomeBodyBeautifulJanelleFletcher

Dancing in Her Own Full Moonlight Women's Circle:

www.facebook.com/groups/DancinginherownFullMoonlight

ACKNOWLEDGEMENT

I am grateful for life challenges that have brought me back to self-love and a connection with my inner feminine power, and my travelling experiences that have helped me discover universal truths that we all simply desire love and inner peace. Thanks also to my family, who have taught me to be bold in realising the "real me," and Spirit, who continues to remind me I am here for a reason.

DEDICATION

To Pierre—my beautiful Frenchman, who has taught me to put myself first, and find courage to keep going on my path. My self-love has never been so bold. Je t'aime.

The Cyclical Wave of Soul
Why I Wasn't a Failure Leaving My Marriage

JANELLE FLETCHER

"Your soul may whisper words you don't wish to hear.

But in honouring that wisdom, you will feel well in your soul."
~Janelle Fletcher

Today is an ending, nine years exactly to the day from a beginning. And it's not surprising that it's the first day of spring, with a feeling of new wind in my sails, as I disembark from the long and often difficult voyage of the past nine years after I left my marriage.

There was once a man called Spafford who endured enormous hardship. His son died at the age of two, and having been a very prosperous lawyer and businessman, when he was struck by the disaster of the Great Chicago Fire of 1872, he suffered financial ruin. Spafford, struggling with the recession that followed the fire, made plans to travel by boat to Europe. Last minute, while attending to some business, he sent his family ahead, but as his wife and children crossed the Atlantic, the ship sank and four of his daughters drowned. Soon after, when crossing the ocean to meet his grieving wife and close to where his daughters found their resting place, he penned this verse of what is now a well-known song: "It is well with my Soul":

When peace like a river, attendeth my way,
When sorrows like sea billows roll
Whatever my lot, thou hast taught me to say
It is well, it is well, with my soul.

Nine years ago today, all was not well with my soul. It was also the day I told each of my six children that I was leaving my marriage. But how could I do this considering mothering was my most-cherished endeavour and I had many years of parenting ahead of me? Externally things seemed pretty calm on the water, but my soul didn't whisper. Instead she shouted deep from within to honour her. Convinced we could work it out, counselling was a consideration, but intuitively, I knew healing the soul ache was the way to face the billows that were rolling.

I awoke a month prior to this difficult family announcement, to the words in my head, "Jump in your car and drive." I didn't know where or why, yet I followed the call. Parking outside a shop, something drew me in and I found myself lying on a table in a healing shop. Within minutes, the purpose of my marriage was revealed, and permission to leave was granted, with me left not feeling a failure, but a woman who had deeply honoured her call, and who was being given a new soul path or wave to ride. Simplistic or unbelievable as it may sound, it was one of my most profound experiences to date, not to mention a spirit-filled reminder that we are asked not to be the controllers of our lives, but instead conduits of spirit. And the bible verse in the third book of Ecclesiastes, "For everything there is a time, a season and a reason," awakened its truth deep within me.

Fourteen years before, I met a widower who had three beautiful young daughters. Within a few months of meeting this man, my first awakening to the spirit world, in stark contrast to my religious upbringing, happened. As we lay together one night, his wife in spirit "spoke" to me as clearly as if she were whispering directly in my ear. Her message was clear. "It's great you two are together. Please take my girls on as your own." A profound message, which I knew was my calling, and one which I graciously and willingly honoured. In that instant, we became not soul-sisters, but soul mothers, with no need for comparison, but united in a bond of jointly loving "our daughters." Within months this widower and I were married and I donned the mantle of instant motherhood. Adding three more children some years later to our happy family, who loved to go camping, travel the world and live life to the full, made the family complete.

So why was I feeling such soul ache and how could I possibly let down the people who mattered most in my world? In fact, my six children were my world, my purpose and my motivation for waking each day. Within moments on the healing table, I was gifted three significant images that revealed the why, and it was then that I instantly made peace with my soul that had previously felt like it was bobbing up and down in a stormy sea.

The first image was of a seven-year-old girl who was crying out, "Mum, don't leave me!" I instantly thought it was my youngest daughter, to whom I feel very connected. Perhaps she could already feel the unrest and stirring within me. The second image was of an American woman, Joni Eareckson Tada, whose songs I had played on the piano in my church community. Joni, as an active teenager, became a quadriplegic after a diving accident. Her creative expression thereafter included singing, painting, writing, and her evangelical mission and work in the disabled community. My second daughter, who sustained a spinal injury in the same car accident that killed her birthmother, was being represented here. Her birth mum, in spirit, was making her message clearer and this daughter was a representation of the older three girls. The third signpost came in the lyrics of the song Joni used to sing and indeed Spafford wrote, "When peace like a river attendeth my way…It is well with my soul."

I was being told, without a doubt, that my mission was complete. I was asked to take on these girls as my own, and ensure they had a safe rite of passage through their grief of losing their mother and transition through their childhood and teenage years until they were "well within their souls" as independent young adults. I had willingly and easily taken on this mission, and done it well. It was also only in hindsight that I could see the parallels between the experience of Spafford, Joni and our family when it came to death, grief, disability and the themes that seem to have threaded their lives and ours.

I was not a failure, nor a victim or a person who wanted to inflict pain on my children or husband, as I announced that I was leaving the marriage. I was, however, committed to aligning with my inner knowing, realising that each of my six children's soul paths were not for me to direct, but I was simply to be the wind in their sails. Spirit was also giving them a new direction that would gift them the life lessons they were to thereafter unwrap and discover for themselves.

Kahlil Gibran penned these words "On Children," which consoled me when I doubted these truths:

Your children are not your children.

They are the sons and daughters of Life's longing for itself.

They come through you but not from you,

And though they are with you yet they belong not to you.

You may give them your love but not your thoughts,
For they have their own thoughts.
You may house their bodies but not their souls,
For their souls dwell in the house of tomorrow,
which you cannot visit, not even in your dreams.
You may strive to be like them,
but seek not to make them like you.
For life goes not backward nor tarries with yesterday.

You are the bows from which your children
as living arrows are sent forth.
The archer sees the mark upon the path of the infinite,
and He bends you with His might
that His arrows may go swift and far.
Let your bending in the archer's hand be for gladness;
For even as He loves the arrow that flies,
so He loves also the bow that is stable.

For sure, I felt immense grief, and even today I well up with tears at the thought of letting go of my ultimate dream of what my mothering, parenting and relationship would look like.

But that real in-touch truth of my spirit—much like a constant travel companion—and my willingness to go beyond my ego, fear, self-judgment or need to control my life, allowed me to step away from what was, to deal with the possible aftermath, the ripples of this change, intact, and face the challenges and soul-growth opportunities that were to come in my next passage in life. Without a doubt, those challenges often wracked me like giant waves crashing against rocks, or pulled me out to sea in the riptide. On occasions, I thought I would drown. But I also felt moments of tranquility when I had the chance to breathe a little before the next wave arrived. Whatever the ocean looked like, however, I managed to stay on board.

My older brother, two years my senior, was celebrating his fortieth in my hometown. My family of birth seldom get together, but this was a special occasion. I was still married, and we both celebrated with my brother and stayed overnight with all of my siblings at his house. A poor sleeper, I was woken, having just had one of only two nightmares in my life. I was on a rollercoaster, careering out of control and unable to brake. I smashed to my death, and I awoke the house with a blood-curdling scream, much like we imagined may have happened in a local murder we were all aware of.

Two years later, it was my fortieth birthday. This time, I celebrated at a different sibling's house. I had exactly the same nightmare—the fun-park, rollercoaster, speed, and the brakes failing, and again I awoke to my own piercing scream and ultimate death. Intuitively, I knew these two nightmares and similar circumstance were no coincidence. Something was to occur that caused "death to myself" at the age of forty and it had to do with family. My separation announcement I gave on the final day, in fact, midnight of the final day of my fortieth year, and the first day of my forty-first.

In just a few days I am celebrating my fiftieth birthday and if one believes in cycles, this nine-year cycle happened to an absolute tee, and I am transitioning midlife into some exciting new travel and adventures with a beautiful new companion and soulmate, my Frenchman. All of my children, whom I am immensely proud of and who are unique treasures, are finding their own inner compass to navigate their way in the world.

In fact, today it is the first day of spring, it's a new moon solar eclipse, as well as my nine-year anniversary, so it is no surprise that peace is in the air and it feels like "smoother sailing." The universe timed it perfectly, and the relief is very welcome. Opportunities have come this week that have long been in the waiting, much like the long-awaited day when you finally go on a trip you have planned for months. Progress with the publication of my book, an ending to a financial commitment, new work opportunities, progress in a business agreement, and the joy of my children coming for my fiftieth birthday dinner are my bounty this week.

Much like Spafford's personal "sea billows" and Joni's "dive into the depths," these nine years certainly provided some large waves, raging rivers and exciting and nerve-wracking times on, and in, the water. I feel the strong pull to write about my unseen struggles, which to others looked like I was staying buoyant throughout. But that would be like turning the ship around and going back to the port of departure, and it would also describe only the troughs of the waves. The crests also looked remarkable, as Spirit calmed and befriended me moment by moment, and I found courage, stillness and even joy in the eye of the storm. It is truly well with my soul.

CHAPTER *Twelve*

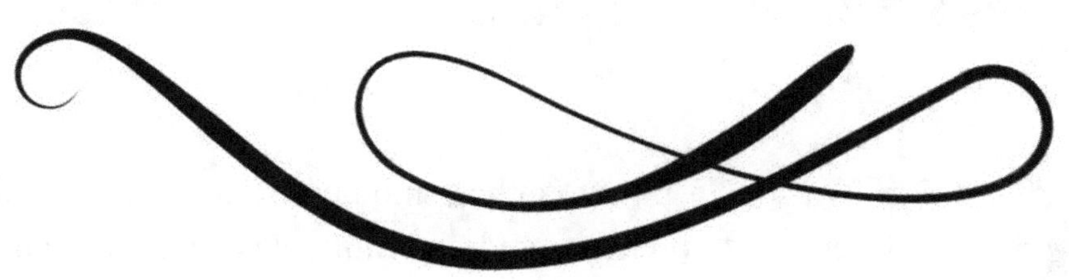

A Journey to Peace

CRISTI TRULSON

Cristi Trulson, aspiring author, mother of three beautiful children, entrepreneur and revolutionary teacher and student of esoteric studies, is currently pursuing certificates in Holistic Life Coaching, Intuition Mastery, and Astrology.

Cristi was born in North Dakota and has many survival skills few appreciate in this day and age. The harsh winter weather builds character and creativity when having to perform daily tasks such as driving, working, and chores to guesstimating the size of a Halloween costume needed to fit over a snowsuit. Besides her sense of humor, she's known for making the best hotdishes and prize-winning slushburgers (ND lingo), pitching hay, and driving anything with a steering device. In her personal life, she has been a business owner and leader in her community; member of her local chamber of commerce, church and 4-H council, SWOT, and Jaycee's, earning many awards for outstanding leadership and excellence from various organizations throughout the state.

Today, she has chosen to use her life lessons (and sarcasm) in conjunction with what she has dubbed 'Tools of the Universe,' to launch an Esoteric Revolution in hopes of dispelling outdated beliefs surrounding these tools and helping others to find a straighter path to peace.

Connect with Cristi

info@esotericrevolution.com

www.esotericrevolution.com

www.facebook.com/esotericrevolution

DEDICATION

This chapter is dedicated to the 'Wolf Pack,' my soul sisters without whom I would not have made it through the darkest of days. My gratitude and love for you is never ending. May you all find peace within and live happily ever after.

ACKNOWLEDGEMENTS

My children are my greatest source for inspiration, unconditional love and support. Thank you for allowing me the space and time to create. In addition, none of this would have been possible without the knowledge and loving guidance I've received from my teacher and publicist Shanda Trofe, for which I will be eternally grateful. Thank you for inviting me on this exciting new path.

A Journey to Peace
Through an Esoteric Revolution?
CRISTI L. TRULSON

Ego says, "Once everything falls into place, I'll find peace."

Spirit says, "Find your peace, and then everything will fall into place.'

~Marianne Williamson

Where to start? Sometimes that's the hardest part. For me, the starting point involved me stopping. It all seems so overwhelming sometimes, like a vicious circle that leads you down and the walls get closer and closer in the descent until you're in a full-blown spin cycle. What amazes me now is how long I used to stay in a place of frustration and negative patterns, in my thoughts, relationships, jobs etc., before moving on. Holding onto things that had long since reached their expiration date was one of my specialties, due to, lack of self-worth, fear of failure, and too much pride. Therefore, I was pouring myself into every vessel around me, expecting it to fill me with the peace I so desperately sought. Sounds silly now, I know. It felt like peace, balance and harmony were outside of me, things I was trying to "get", to acquire. So I had to stop. I had to find what was left of me, come to peace with what was, and find a different way to live.

"Peace is not merely a distant goal we seek,
But a means by which we
arrive at that goal."
~Martin Luther King Jr

It felt as though I had sacrificed my life for the greater goals of security, monetary and personal; happiness for my children; and all the things I thought would bring me happiness and peace. With each passing year I became more confused as bottled up frustration, turned into anger, and suppressed emotions were popping up as negative projections on all the people in my life. I could no longer identify with them, I hated my job(s), my marriage was all but over, my health was failing and worst of all, I had created a chaotic, detached, unorganized and dysfunctional home life for my children.

"We can never obtain peace in the outer
world until we make peace with ourselves."
~Dali Lama

It wasn't until I stopped chasing all those things outside of myself that I was able to start loving myself unconditionally, moving towards a more peaceful existence. Learning to follow my dreams and conquer my goals in a more self-loving way, changed everything. Life didn't have to be hard. I didn't need to seek peace, I already had it. Peace wasn't the goal; it's what I needed to reach my goals. It's true what they say, about loving yourself before you can love another. It's the same with peace. When you are waging a war inside, it's very difficult to spread peace into the world.

The definition of peace is: freedom from disturbance; quiet and tranquility. "Quiet and tranquility" were not easily come by in my house! I started my journey by taking some time each day, away from the chaos of kids, school, critters, farming, working, and volunteering, to stop and just be still. To breathe. I soon realized, I had created all the 'busy-ness' to keep from seeing what was really going on. I saw a life that left no room for me, my growth or my identity. I was sad, angry and taking it out on the world around me.

The freedom from disturbance that gives you the time to sit with yourself, with no one else in a room full of mirrors, isn't exactly a good time either. I had avoided this room for years. I couldn't think of anything worse than owning my part of the failure and sadness I brought to others. I had to get brave enough to forgive all my judgements and wrong doings, and most importantly, forgive myself.

"Inner peace can be reached only when we practice forgiveness. Forgiveness is letting go of the past, and therefore the means for correcting our misperceptions."
~Gerald Jampolsk

FORGIVENESS=PEACE

I wrote it everywhere, so I would remember, because the LAST thing I was prepared to do was to forgive, anyone, especially myself, but I did. Releasing all that anger and pain brought a great sense of relief. And the most beautiful part of letting it all go and forgiving yourself is that all those judgements you feared and worries you held are gone, it is so freeing!! I then started encouraging myself with positive reinforcements, and expressing my gratitude for small everyday things I once over looked. And a sense of peace started to grow, in the same place fear had been.

Learn what makes you happy, and makes your light shine! Forgive yourself, and all others. Love yourself, and all others. We are all beautiful bright souls, fighting our egos, and searching for love. Let's shine our lights out into the world!

Let Peace Grow in You

Cultivate the seed of Peace within you
Nurture with positive thoughts & self-love
Water with tears of Gratitude & Forgiveness
Nourish with an abundance of Love & Wisdom
Strengthen with Fortitude & Grace
Watch it bloom through acts of Compassion & Kindness
Once the bloom begins to fade, be the winds of change
That carry its seed…
Let's all strive to be the winds of change that carry the seed of peace and plant it along our path.

The following are some tips and tools from experts, in their respective fields, all of which are an integral part on my journey to peace. There is of course, so much more information available, but these are methods, teachers and people I trust and often refer others to. The following are just a few of the fun and helpful techniques I used to keep a positive attitude, find my truth, and help me become a better person. With greatest respect to all belief systems and truths to which you adhere, my hope is that you may find a tool that resonates with you and can assist you on your journey.

One of the first things I discovered was the Law of Attraction movement. It gave me such hope and a sense that I was still steering this vessel and had some control over its direction. This law taught me to let go of negative thought patterns and needless worries, which in and of itself was a positive change in my life. I started to see that thoughts do become things and adhering to positive thoughts and eliminating that which is not in alignment with your soul, can make miracles happen. Esther Hicks, of Abraham-Hicks Publication, is a delight to listen to and her humor is a wonderful bonus to her very spot-on, simple and consistent answers to what seem like such complicated problems. *The Secret* by Rhonda Byrne was one of the first books I read and I remember thinking "There is no way it could be THIS easy!" Well, it's not easy to stay positive and trust in the universe nonstop! But…there is magic in it when you do! *Notes from the Universe* by Mike Dooley, is uplifting as well. He delivers a short, encouraging daily email that some days, makes all the difference in the world! They are strangely synchronistic with your personal life events and it's free! You'll find a wealth of information on all three websites; articles, books, videos, classes, retreats.

Another fool proof way of releasing old thought patterns is by showing our gratitude! Being grateful every day for all our blessings is the quickest way to finding more of them. If the only thing you change today is, writing 10 things you are grateful for, morning and night, you will be amazed by what changes in your life! I can't tell you how many days I felt like I had nothing to be grateful for. Our minds are strong and sometimes it's difficult to remember our blessings. Save your lists and read them on the difficult days, as a reminder of all you have.

"Astrology is a science in itself and contains
an illuminating body of knowledge.
It taught me many things
and I am greatly indebted to it."
~Albert Einstein

We have established that the true journey to peace begins within, and what better way to know yourself than to obtain the 'Blue print of your Soul'! It has been the most valuable tool I have found for understanding myself, loved ones, friends and foe alike. Once you know the placement of just a couple planets, it's easy to understand how and why you react to certain situations and what makes you happy and gives you peace. When you take a more in-depth look or have an astrologer explain your natal chart to you, I believe you will be pleasantly surprised at how deeply it resonates with your soul. It is much more than reading your horoscope in a paper; there is a beauty and truth in this knowledge unlike any other.

The Sun represents your personal identity, your ego and your unique self-expression. If you don't identify with your sun sign, you may be on a cusp i.e.; where one sign ends and another begins. Then you may take on the qualities of both signs. Many people also identify with their rising sign (sign on the ascendant) as this is the way others perceive you, it is how you interact socially and view and react to people. The Moon helps define our emotional development, or express the unconscious side of our personality. The New Moon is the perfect time each month to set new goals; a powerful time to plant new seeds of intention and watch as they grow, when the moon becomes full. The Full Moon is the perfect time for celebration if you are reaping the rewards of the seeds planted on the New Moon, or letting go of things that no longer serve you. The Full Moon will cast its light on the situation, good or bad, and bring it to your attention.

Mercury defines our mind; thoughts, communications, and the way we use them. Venus represents the qualities of love, romance, sensuality, culture, beauty and affection we seek and give. The red planet, Mars, indicates impulsiveness, aggressiveness, courageousness, and how we put action and will-power to use! Jupiter symbolizes expansion, development and good fortune, it can also tell you where you tend to over extend or go too far. Saturn is the task-master, and like grandfather time teaches us the important lessons through experiences, challenges and situations that aren't always fun, but put us on the right track. Uranus is the planet of rebellion, cutting-edge technology, future events and like lightening, you never know where it may strike! Pluto may be the smallest, but it's in charge of the big stuff; transformation, regeneration and rebirth. There is so much more the celestial bodies can teach us, about our wounds, strengths and purpose.

Another favorite tool, dating back to 6th century BC and Pythagoras, is Numerology, the study of numbers, and the manner in which they reflect certain skills and character tendencies, as part of the universal plan. Each letter has a numeric value that provides a related cosmic vibration. The sum of the numbers in your birth date and the sum of value derived from the letters in your name provide an interrelation of vibrations. These numbers reveal character, purpose in life, what motivates, and where talents may lie. Experts in numerology use the numbers to determine the best time for major moves and activities in life. I was shocked at how accurate my life path number was! There are numerous books on this subject and again, it's a fun way to see yourself in a new light.

Are you an extrovert or introvert? Do you think or feel more? Do you judge or perceive? The Myers-Briggs Foundation has developed a personality type indicator known as MTBI, described here per their website, myersbriggs.org, "*The purpose of the Myers-Briggs Type Indicator® (MBTI®) personality inventory is to make the theory of psychological types described by C. G. Jung understandable and useful in people's lives. The essence of the theory is that much seemingly random variation in the behavior is actually quite orderly and consistent, due to basic differences in the ways individuals prefer to use their perception and judgment.*"

I'm an orange! I'd never been called THAT before! As luck would have it, that fateful day of travel, I was seated right next to a nice young man whose mother just happens to be the creator of *Essential Colors.* Shortly after our initial introductions, he decided I was an Orange. I couldn't wait to land and take the short quiz and learn more, turns out he was right! Here is a bit more information per their website myessentialcolors.com

"Essential Colors communication firm is built on the personality model of 4 personality types that dates back to 420 B.C. Dr. Sabrina Jackson found how these 4 personality types relate to the bible, the universe, and people's problems through research. She used several past scholars work to help inspire her own model such as; The Bible, Myers-Briggs, True Colors Intl, and more. Essential Colors is striving to be the leader in instruction of how people can effectively work together. This is a worldwide conversation proven to train all facets of people to effectively generate results amongst each other, using a quantitative self-assessment. Essential Colors was designed to grant participants more access to improve results within businesses, faith based organizations, schools, and personal relationships."

"The canvas of life... is waiting...for some bright colours...

"Let us add shades of Joy, Love, Peace and Happiness..."
~Rishika Jain

> *"Our hearts resonate at the same frequency as the earth and the universe. Therefore, we are all valuable instruments in the orchestration of the world and its harmony. We must always be aware of the vibrations we emit individually and collectively. Always be in command of your music. Only you can control and shape its tone. If life throws you a few bad notes or vibrations, don't let them interrupt or alter your song."*
>
> *— Suzy Kassem*

It's no secret that our bodies are made up of energy fields. Energy fuels your body's internal functions, repairs, builds and maintains cells and body tissues, and supports the external activities that enable you to interact with the physical world. Water, your body's most important nutrient, helps facilitate the chemical reactions that produce energy from food. I have found energy healing work to be most beneficial. Regularly practicing Chakra healing techniques and Reiki are powerful ways to balance the energy body and create vibrant health on every level. I have also used EFT technique. The Emotional Freedom Techniques (EFT) is a form of psychological acupressure that uses tapping with the finger-tips on specific points on the face and body to clear emotional issues. Body Talk is a similar energy medicine that has seen much success.

I think once we dig deeper into finding our core selves, center our bodies and open our minds to all the diverse tools available, we can come to an understanding that we are all unique individuals and perfect just as we are. There is much peace in that.

"It is wisdom to know others; it is enlightenment to know one's self."
~Lao-Tzu

The purpose behind this book is to put some positive energy back into a world that seems anything but peaceful. Being a positive light and spreading positive energy is a valuable tool. We can always find a way to justify our position on almost any topic, but if we don't step back and look at the whole picture, we lose sight of the original purpose, the solution. In a world of constant chaos and illusion, a non-stop media stream of strangeness and absurdity unlike we've ever seen on this planet, it's hard to get a grasp on reality. Even reality TV, isn't real. You don't have to look too far if you're itching for a fight or want something to feel bad about with race wars, a political freak show, the good guys being bad guys, more opinions than answers, protests and riots everywhere, the list goes on and on. Like I was doing, we've become so accustomed to reaching for things outside of ourselves to find something to stand for, an identity to cling to, yet we find ourselves in constant opposition to those who believe otherwise. To fulfill the need to belong, we must tap into a place we don't remember, to the peace we knew before we became separated and were taught what to believe, a time before we formed our jaded perceptions in an ego-driven world. Unlearn all that; look within and see how unique you are. Maybe if we stopped fighting about inconsequential things and started fighting for our personal truth, we would find unity, find the light we all bear and shine it into the darkness of this sad world, and come together. Making the choice to choose positive thoughts, actions and deeds for the benefit of all, in each moment, is an important step in finding a solution to shifting our journey and staying on a path of Peace.

NAMESTA

"I honor the place in you in which the entire universe dwells.

I honor the place in you which is of love, of truth, of light, and of peace.

When you are in that place in you and I am in that place in me, we are one."

"To transform the world, we must begin with ourselves, and what is important in beginning with ourselves is the intention. The intention must be to understand ourselves and not to leave it to others to transform themselves or to bring about a modified change through revolution, either of the left or of the right. It is important to understand that this is our responsibility, yours and mine;

"Because, however small may be the world we live in, if we can transform ourselves, bring about a radically different point of view in our daily existence, then perhaps we shall affect the world at large, the extended relationship with others."
~J.Krishnamurti

CHAPTER

Thirteen

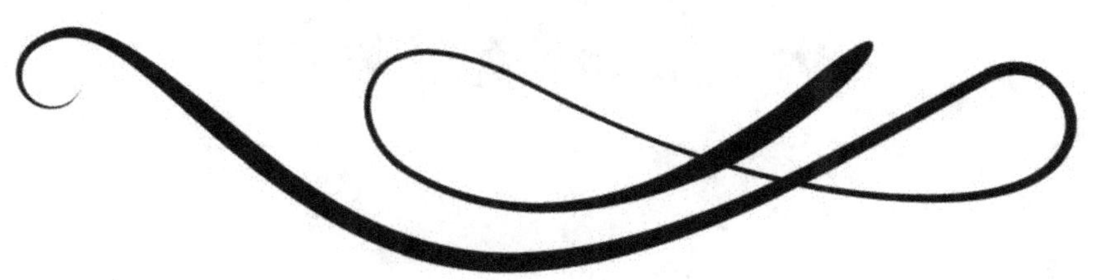

Sayoko-San

My Peacemaker Mama

JULIE SANDERS

Julie Sanders is a professional Psychic and Medium practicing in Sonoma County, California since 1999. At the age of 5, Julie's daughter Jazmine came up with the name for her website, The Heart Of The Spirit explaining, "Mommy, that is you." Appropriately named for Julie possesses a unique ability and talent for unraveling and reframing feelings and out dated beliefs for her clients.

In living through and healing a series of traumatic relationships Julie embodies compassion and insight that allows her to be a voice of experience. Her goal in private sessions is to provide the client with a direct connection to their inner knowing. Her desire to connect people to their innocence frees them from remaining connected to their self-judgment of their past choices. The overall experience is one of comfort and empowerment. Clients describe that their sessions bring them great comfort and clarity.

It is not uncommon for a session to incorporate various modalities of healing. Trained as a Shamanic Practitioner, Hypnotherapist and Aura Soma Practitioner, Julie draws on her wide background in metaphysical training. A session may include work on a Past Life issue as the entirety of the soul experience receives equal attention and is valued as a part of bringing the client to a place of wholeness and grace.

ACKNOWLEDGMENT

My mother, Jan Sanders blazed a trail for me and my brothers that allowed us to become the full actualized versions of who our souls yearned to be. With her unconditional and unwavering support; she taught me the value of listening and being truly present. I am so blessed to have her as my best friend and soul mate in this lifetime.

DEDICATION

I dedicate this chapter to my children, Ben, Nick and Jazmine. During my darkest hours, their love buoys me through. Each of them possess their unique brand of wisdom and they truly make a difference in the world. They are my pride and joy.

Sayoko-San

My Peacemaker Mama

JULIE SANDERS

From the kitchen I hear my mother humming and break out into song, quietly singing to herself in what may well have been a part of her spiritual practice. “Let there be peace on earth and let it begin with me…”* Throughout my childhood mom sought to bring peace not only to her past but into the lives of all she met. A true peace-nick and semi-hippy mama, she had us recycling and meditating long before the wave of self-awareness was the booming phenomena it is today. I remember hearing her say that she was going to register my brothers as Conscientious Objectors to prevent them from having to go to war. The Vietnam war was in full swing during my childhood but thank God, it ended before my brothers came of age to be drafted.

My mother is third generation Japanese American. At the age of 8 her home and childhood were taken from her and her family – in the name of war. Over the years I have asked her to write down her story, the fascinating history of her own life. Despite my curiosity and fascination, she has resisted saying essentially that she is not that story. It has long been my desire to know every tiny detail of what it felt like to lose your home and be placed into a refurbished horse stall with only whitewash covering the remains of horse manure, awaiting shipment out. I wondered what did it feel like to be whisked away from life as she knew it and put in a concentration camp with barbed wire? These questions remain unanswered to my inquiring mind. Why wasn’t she furious? Why doesn't she want to tell her story? That's a very good question and I will do my best to embrace her experience.

From the time she was young, my mother Sayoko (Sayoko-san would be a term of endearment) had a feisty streak. While the world may have told her she was powerless, she turned to her rich inner world of faith. No, she probably did not call it faith at that time. What my mother possesses, that cannot be taken from her, is insatiable curiosity. Her curiosity, I believe, is what protected her from buying into a story that she was a victim of some governmental act. Time at camp was a bit of an adventure to this very bright young girl. If you ever want to know about life, strip away the trappings of comfort and see where you are left. Luckily for mom, she was good company to herself and did not waste time on self-pity.

During my childhood mom fed her curiosity reading progressive thinkers like Edgar Cayce and Carl Jung. Unlike other moms, she didn't dally around with gossip, the PTA or playing bridge. Mom had a calling from the metaphysical realm. She got her answers by tossing three pennies and asking the I Ching her important questions and received spiritual sustenance from this ancient Book of Change. Around the age of 13 she taught me how to read the hexagrams and I would ask my silly 13-year-old girl questions. Does so and so like me? Will I make get selected for cheerleader? What I know now, is that even though my questions were superficial, this was my initiation into mysticism and spirituality. As I look back I see that this was preparation to my spiritualty and my future as an intuitive reader.

Throughout our childhood she sprinkled us with consciousness beyond what made sense at the time – to my brothers and I. In the early days we would rinse out cans, remove the labels and flatten them to be recycled…how embarrassing…really mom? Everybody else just threw theirs in the garbage, not us! Recycling was not optional because mom was not going to litter mother earth with garbage for us kids to inherit. Mind you this was in the 1960's! We were taught to respect mother earth. I recognize that she always had a higher calling and was unafraid to put her spiritual practices and earthly responsibilities into her household.

My mother was unapologetic about her rituals. As a teenager I was often embarrassed about her rituals. Another totally embarrassing thing she did was make homemade bread…all I wanted was Wonder Bread. Nope! She would time her baking so that the bread would be hot out of the oven when we arrived home from school, knowing the house would smell amazing and we could have a snack of fresh bread. Feeding was one of her go-to medicines. My older brother Jeff and I had friends from broken families. Divorce was uncommon in the 1960's. As a child I didn't understand that my friends didn't get fed like we did. Our dinner table often had extra hungry mouths to feed, and mom was in her element. Maybe part of her desire to feed these hungry kids was born of her past in the concentration camp, but if it was, she never admitted it. My peace-nick earth mama loved to feed those children that she felt needed nourishment. There are still kids from my childhood that recall her kind and loving nature and most especially her food! Mom taught us that generosity is always possible, she used to tell me, "There's always enough honey." She was right. Raising my children, our table was the one with extra mouths to feed. Providing a loving environment for kids that may not have that at home was a passion for me. There were many who came for dinner, and many who came and stayed, some for days, and some for weeks. Whether they stayed for dinner or longer, feeding them created a bond between me and the children that lives forever in my heart.

When I was fourteen my dad got transferred 60 miles north of my childhood home. I truly felt that I would die. My whole childhood, all my friends and our family home were gone. What I didn't realize was that this move was an opportunity to learn about who I had grown to be under my mom's gentle upbringing. You see, we didn't have a lot of rules at home, there was really only one; be thoughtful of others and their feelings. If we were caught not living up to this our punishment was not to be grounded, no it was something far more challenging; Mom would sit us down and make us think about what we did and how it might have made the other person feel. Consciousness building. She was consistent. My brothers and I would joke that we just received lecture 127 or lecture 251…we'd giggle and she knew it but I'll tell you, there were plenty of times I would have preferred to be sent to my room and not have to look at my actions through my mother's lens. During these times of "punishment" she taught us how to think for ourselves and also, that we would not escape accountability. There was no wiggle room, you'd sit and listen and have to engage your mind and heart. Consistent with mom's peaceful nature, she was never punitive and punishment was never arbitrary, it was never more than engaging with whichever lecture I was receiving.

The result of my mother's method of training us to engage our hearts and minds, was three people who think for themselves and have no problem questioning authority. Yeah, that was part of the lesson plan. These were the days where children were expected to respect our elders. Many elders still held to the archaic belief that children were to be seen and not heard. Whelp…we were not those children. Our mother instructed us that we only had to respect that which is respectable! Aha! Loophole! But alas, no loophole. Bottom line was that because we had been taught to be thoughtful of others and their feelings. We were respectful even to those who did not warrant it. What I learned is that kindness to someone who is unkind has a way of softening their edges. Wow! This was a huge revelation!

As we matured the life lessons we were faced with changed as well. I remember complaining to mom about someone and wanted nothing more than for her to join my team and agree with me!

"Honey, I read something once that said; the person who seems to deserve the love the least needs it the most." Dang, really mom? Do you really have a kind explanation for everything in life? So what you're telling me is that this person with horrid behavior needs a hug? Time and again her commitment to peaceful resolution of any and all situations bore out to be true. The lesson of compassion taught through recognizing bad behavior as internal pain is a big gigantic tool in my tool box of life. I didn't learn it all at once as my ego really wanted to be pissed off. Heck, sometimes I even wanted to be the victim! I wanted mom to jump up and down and defend me! I later understood that she did in fact protect me…in her own unique way.

When something came up a school, she was "Johnny on the spot" to let the faculty know that they absolutely did not have permission to paddle her children! I'm pretty sure the principal would cringe when he saw her coming…this of course made us giggle… And there were also times she did not jump up and defend me, she would create a whole new lecture to fit the circumstances and I would once again, have to think and feel my way to a peaceful conclusion of my own design. She never gave us the answers, but she gave us the confidence to seek them out on our own.

At 85 years old my precious mother's faith continues to amaze me. She told me once that she decided to always trust us kids. So when we'd make some silly decision, she'd say, "I trust you honey, you'll know just what to do." I guess it's good that she trusted us even though we were normal teenagers doing normal teenage antics, it probably saved her a few grey hairs! I adopted this in raising my children as well. It was empowering to them to know that I believed in their life skills and problem solving ability. As a parent I would still give guidance when asked, I am a mom after all – that's in the mom play book. I emulated my mom's teaching and gave my children the gift of my trust, which in turn gave them the confidence that even if they made a bad decision, they could figure a way out of it. In reality, there have been many times I worried and fretted over my children and their choices until I remember the antidote to fear, which is what my mother had been teaching us all about all along, faith, "Don't fight every battle, don't take everything personally, and let things play out and see where you stand." Letting things play out is allowing faith and grace to fill in the spaces of what we do not know.

The last mom-ism I would love to give you is a gift she gave me often growing up. As a young girl there were really scary things happening in the Bay Area. There was a serial killer – I was very afraid. The police couldn't find him and he seemed to be in control of my feelings of security. The mom balm I received was something she repeated often; "You are always safe and protected." I heard it so often that it became part of the tape that played in the background of my mind. She would occasionally offer more words of comfort such as, "this is not part of your reality honey," or "some people are here to learn lessons about violence, but not you."

I am truly grateful for the opportunity to share the story of my mother's incredible influence on all who she has touched. When she said she didn't need to tell the story about the concentration camp because it wasn't her story, I get it now. Her story is and always has been about faith, hope, kindness and love. She walked her talk and continues to inspire me to know that in spite of what the world may be doing, I am always safe and protected. As the most profound peacemaker in my life, she would want you to know that you too, are always safe and protected.

*"**Let There Be Peace on Earth**" written by Jill Jackson Miller and Sy Miller in 1955.

CHAPTER Fourteen

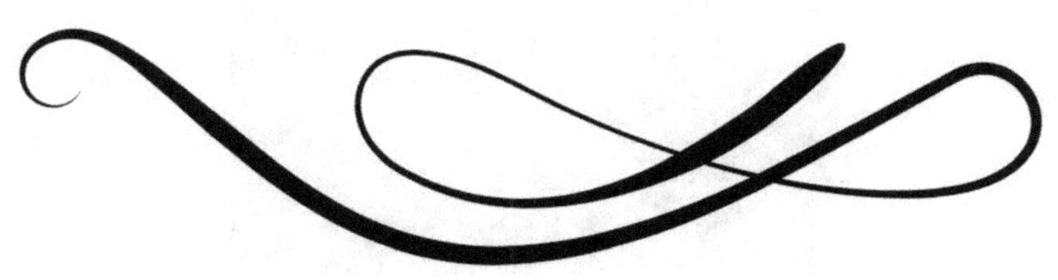

Acts of Unconditional Love

VANESSA THIBEAULT

Vanessa is the mother of two intelligent little girls who keep her on her toes. She is working towards her Bachelor of Arts degree through Thompson Rivers University, with a major in English. She currently runs a daycare from her home as well as facilitates 0-6 programs in her community. Vanessa spends her days reading, gardening, and making memories with her children. Vanessa spends many of her evenings with close friends enjoying good wine and conversation. She would like to travel and explore the world one day. She currently resides in Southern British Columbia with its warm summers and mild winters, where she can experience the joys of the outdoors.

DEDICATION

Dedicated to those I have loved, those I love now and all whom I will love in the future.

ACKNOWLEDGEMENT

Thank you to L.R. for helping me to find my strength in words; thank you to D.K. for teaching me about the beauty that lives in everyday life; thank you to K.G. for showing me how to have faith in myself. Your confidence and love have helped me find my way.

Acts of Unconditional Love

VANESSA THIBEAULT

Love for Others

Life often throws us twists and turns we could never have imagined. We lose those close to us, or we are the ones who become lost. For some, these losses leave us hardened and selfish. Self-reflection gets thrown in a pile at the back of our room, in a forgotten heap of broken promises and unmet expectations. We forget to love; we forget how to love. When we neglect what should be the very basis of our being, we forget how to act, and from where our actions should originate. Our actions should be born of love: love for each other and for ourselves.

Many people would argue that there are no truly selfless acts. They say every motivation has an element that benefits the giver. Although this may be true in principle, there are many ways in which giving and acting out of love leaves the giver with less than the receiver. Think of a parent caring for their child. There are many sacrifices that a parent makes for their child from which they receive little or no gain. Parents' love and responsibility for their child is what drives them to sleepless nights, countless tears, tireless efforts and the denial of their own wants and even needs.

Ultimately, actions done out of love are selfless. Responsibility doesn't give room for choice, and when you combine love and responsibility, your actions will have the right intentions. Oftentimes, though, pride gets in our way.

Allowing our actions to be guided by love is more difficult than we think. This is because we may lack the ability to self-reflect on how our fears are preventing us from truly loving one another. When we experience fear, we inhibit our ability to love.

We've all been hurt and let down, sometimes by the very people who, by their relationship to us, should have provided us support. As individuals, we have no control over those events, but we can control who we become after those events. Understanding those who have hurt us, how they must in turn be hurting to treat us with such disregard, allows us to release ourselves from the grip of the anger that holds us.

"Hurt people, hurt people..."

-Will Bowen

When we allow ourselves to be released from our pain, we will no longer feel the need to inflict pain. We will then be able to base our actions on love, thereby changing the world from the one we see today.

Love for Ourselves

We are often so concerned about how we are perceived by others that we forget about nurturing ourselves. We do not want to come off as selfish or self-serving. We want to be seen as self-sacrificing and giving. As mothers we give and give until we have nothing left, but often mothers are reminded of one important premise of motherhood: to take care of our children we must also, and sometimes even first, take care of ourselves. Why is it that the only time we are given the advice to look after ourselves is when we are at the brink of complete exhaustion?

When do you push your needs aside for someone else's?
Do you validate and defend these behaviors in any way?

____

____

____

____

This is a conversation we should start with each of our children, not just our daughters (though I used the example of mothers taking care of themselves in the example above), long before they are burdened with responsibilities; long before we are in the exhausted, tapped-out state that so many of us are in today. Imagine a world where people took care of themselves first, instead of stretching themselves so thin they have nothing to give to anyone else. People would be patient with each other; we would listen to each other; none of us would feel guilt for taking time to unwind and rejuvenate. We would not have to fear being perceived as self-serving because we are doing what is best for us. Because what is best for us, ultimately, is best for all.

"To say 'I love you' one must know first how to say the 'I.'"
~Ayn Rand, The Fountainhead

We need to teach our children that it is ok to take time for ourselves. And that this will encourage self-reflection. And self-reflection leads us to a higher consciousness where we can fully give of ourselves. Upon self-reflection we allow ourselves to become aware of our misgivings, insincerities, insecurities and fears. All of these detract from our ability to act out of love. If we can teach our children how to self-reflect from a young age, what a world we will raise! And the best way to teach a child is to lead by example.

List three things you can do to show yourself that you care about yourself right now.

1. ____

2. ____

3. ____

If you chose to do something just for you each day,

do you think your life would change? Remember, it can be as simple as watching

the sunset, or drinking your favorite coffee.

____

____

____

____

Any action done out of love can have no bad intentions; when actions are based on fear, pain, jealousy, greediness or selfishness, they bring about the same feelings in the recipient of the actions. When an action is performed in love that is selfless, that act breeds love. Perform Actions of Unconditional Love today! See how your life will change; watch how the lives of those around you will change as well.

List three areas in your life where you could start to practice 'Actions of Unconditional Love.'

1. ____

2. ____

3. ____

Implement them in your life today!

CHAPTER

A Peaceful End to Conflict

JODIE HARVALA

Jodie Harvala is a forward thinking, spirit loving, space clearing, psychic teacher and coach. She is also the founder of The Spirit School. Walking through her own spirit journey she went from a fear *based* woman to a Spiritually FearLESS entrepreneur.

Jodie loves teaching others how to connect with spirit and also how to experience spirit in the sacred, everyday moments of life. She teaches through experience. With each and every class offered, people who participate walk away with their own very real experience with spirit and a fresh perspective regarding the next step on their personal journey here on earth.

Jodie shares tools and ideas to connect with spirit on a daily basis, creating your own magical experiences day to day. When we walk through life with direction from spirit, we become fearless. With each course offered at The Spirit School, you will feel more empowered and filled with magic in your own life. Hands on your hearts, ladies and gentleman. It's time to pledge allegiance to your higher self. All aboard the bus to The Spirit School!

Connect with Jodie

Jodie@JodieHarvala.com

www.JodieHarvala.com

www.TheSpiritSchool.com

DEDICATION

To my boys—always.

ACKNOWLEDGEMENTS

I would like to acknowledge every single person who shows up in my life to teach me to be a more peaceful human being.

A Peaceful End to Conflict

JODIE HARVALA

Have you ever worked with horses or heard of the Equine Gestalt Coaching Method? My prior experience with horses was limited and not full of fond memories. Our relatives had a beautiful farm near Bismarck, ND and a few horses we rode occasionally. One particularly unpleasant memory stands out from the rest. I can still clearly picture being on the back of a horse that was running full speed towards the barn. Little 11-year-old me was terrified!

The horse saw the barn and was ready to go home – so that's what it did. Full speed. Me screaming. Full stop with me almost flying off and uttering what was most likely my first swear word said in front of adults. Not the best memory of the beautiful creatures!

From that moment on I kept my distance. Yes, they were beautiful. Yes, they had pretty eyes. Yes, the smell of a barn is something I am fond of. No, I'd rather not get much closer.

That was until I met Sarah. A wacky, funny woman I met through an Expo a few years ago. She has this really fun laugh and the energy around her felt very interesting to me. Throughout the day as I heard more and more about her horses and her work, the more intrigued I became.

"You don't ride the horses??? What do you mean they help you with clients? You don't ride them? I don't get it."

Sarah explained Gestalt therapy and something inside said 'just go for it - have a session.'

I love new experiences so I showed up with my mud boots & jeans and excitement for the day. As we went to say hi to the horses she looked out in the field and said "Really, Blue?" hmmm ok. Of course my high alert was up at that point.

I was brought into the arena and after going through important safety measures we went to work. A huge beautiful horse named Lance entered the pen with me and I immediately began shaking. I was incredibly scared of this horse - he was HUGE. I was told that being scared of horses often means you may be afraid of your own power. Sarah also told me to speak with the horses with total honesty. 'You are beautiful but I am scared out of my mind!' was a comment Lance heard often.

As I became more comfortable with big ole Lance my confidence was building as well. Sarah put a broom handle down on the ground and asked me to stand on one side. Lance immediately strolled over the other side and stared me down.

As I sat on my side of the broom with this huge animal staring me down with those peaceful eyes I started to cry and had no idea why. Sarah gently coached me saying the side I was standing on was my human-self. Lance was standing in for my spirit-self. I knew I had been feeling so much conflict inside myself and walked with it most of my life. I had wanted to work on that because so much conflict was showing up in my outside life too.

Suddenly, I was crying and angry. Sarah encouraged me to communicate with Lance and tell him why I was crying and angry. "I'm exhausted. I'm tired. I don't feel heard. I'm so angry. I don't trust my spirit."

WHAT?!

All of these emotions and words fell out of me and with each one my body felt lighter. I couldn't believe what I was saying and yet it rang true. Somehow this horse saw inside me.

Then, it was time to switch. Before I even took a step Lance was making his way to the other side of the broom. Did I tell you horses are incredibly intuitive and fantastic lie detectors? As I stepped onto my spirit side, my energy shot up and my strength was tenfold. It was the wildest thing I had ever felt! It was like I was free!

Lance again stared me down and nudged me a bit with his nose. I had this intuitive hit that he was saying my human side also felt like my spirit was pushy. Yes. I could feel that. My spirit had many things to say to my human side. Most of all, spirit also didn't feel heard and really had wanted to have more of a partnership. So the inner conflict I had always felt was my spirit-self and my human-self fighting. Can you relate?

It was one of the most clarifying experiences I have ever had.

Then we moved on to Blue. Blue, the big red horse. He had this beautiful reddish hair and I noticed right away he was pretty sassy. He even was nibbling on Sarah a bit. I immediately remembered a friend of mine who had been bitten by a horse and left with this huge bruise.

No thank you!

Sarah was telling me about Blue and I doing a trust walk and again the horse was biting at her. I started to have my freak out moment, saying I was not walking with a horse that bites.

I swear he looked right at me and tried to bite her again! I said, "SEE! He did that on purpose! No way am I walking with that horse and I can't believe you're even asking me to!" She dug in her heels. "Tell me why Jodie."

"Because I don't trust that damn horse and I sure as hell don't trust you now!"

Commence major FREAK OUT! Tears and swearing and all the fun that goes with a freak out on a big horse named Blue, who was really red.

Then something came over me – a moment of calm and I swear someone said to take a breath. So I did. I stopped, I took a breath. I said, "Fine I will do it. But if he bites me I will never forgive you." Sarah – a complete professional – took a breath with me. She said, "We can do this Jodie." I took that rope and off we went. Blue pushed me around a bit and our circle took a turn for the worst. I started to panic. I walked over to Sarah to get help and she said "No, you can do this. Take control of him. You are the boss!"

I was not happy with her but I looked at that horse and I decided, screw it we are going to figure this out! I turned around and all of a sudden Sarah said, "Wait a second. Drop the rope. Do the same trust walk but no rope - just ask him to walk alongside you."

Again, I swear this happened. Blue, the big red horse, looked at me and said take a breath. We both took a huge, clearing breath and he looked at me again and said let's do this. And we walked. We walked a perfect circle several times and understood each other and worked well together. I fell in love with that horse in that moment! I was so proud of myself. Sarah just watched with a big ole smile on her face.

I went from being incredibly frightened of horses to feeling so powerful. To date, it is one of my favorite types of work I have done on self-growth. I really enjoyed every part of it once I understood what I was doing.

Here are a few things that took me a few weeks to integrate.

- I was afraid of my power – Lance showed me the way to have a healthy respect for my inner power.
- I was afraid to trust – I didn't trust myself, my power or my spirit so how could anyone else trust me?
- I didn't listen – again, I wasn't hearing myself, my power or my spirit. Why should anyone else listen if I wasn't?

The biggest lesson was about Blue, the big red horse. Blue was ME. He was a direct reflection of myself and I had no idea. He was sassy and stubborn and didn't like anyone leading him around but most of all he was MISUNDERSTOOD.

I found out later Blue was not always the choice to do these types of sessions because he was a little unpredictable & sassy and yes, pushy. That made me laugh because I knew some people felt exactly the same way about me. The best part was I got new understanding about myself and Sarah learned some new tips for working with Blue and now understood him better too.

He does way better when you drop the rope and just let him do his work! Yes, Blue…me too!

The more I understand myself, the more peaceful I feel within myself. This book is all about stories of peace. My story shows how creating peace within creates peace on the outside world too. The conflict that was so present in my life almost disappeared. Of course I still have my moments but I don't live in it any longer. Peace within – Peace in the world!

CHAPTER Sixteen

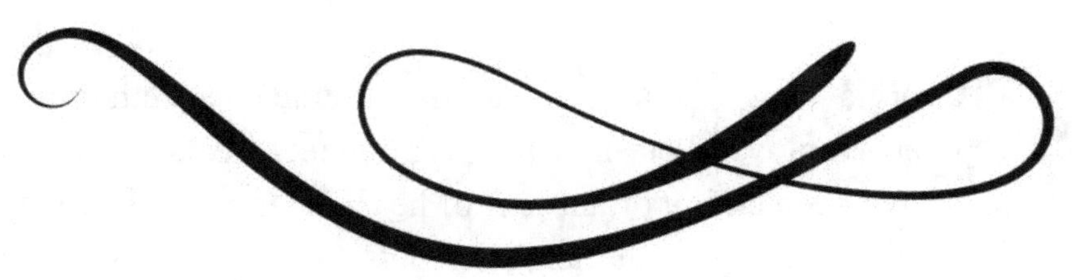

Unconditional Love

GEORGIA NAGEL

Georgia Nagel is an Animal Communicator, author and self-employed Pet Sitter for over eighteen years. Animals have been an important part of her life for more than fifty years. While working with her own pets and pet clients, she learned of her abilities to communicate with animals present and with those passed on. Georgia loves to educate people on their pets and what they can do to make their lives better by interacting with them. She is presently writing a book on this subject, *Pet Talker (Listening to those who speak silently)*.

In addition to working with animals, Georgia is involved with the local Humane Society and working on developing a reading program for children to read to cats at the shelter. She is also a Certified Invoking the Archangels Practitioner and has undertaken a two-year course with a Shaman on becoming a Shaman Practitioner to further her abilities in working with animals.

CONNECT WITH GEORGIA

Email: gnagel@arvig.net

Website:

www.WhoLetsYourDogsOut.net

Social Media

www.facebook.com/georgianagel

ACKNOWLEDGEMENT

I am thankful to have the love and support of my life-partner Jeff, my mother, sister, brother, nieces, nephews and friends. They may not understand fully what I do, but they encourage and support me always. Finally, I acknowledge Shanda Trofe and the encouragement, knowledge, and kindness she offered in her writing course, where I gained the confidence to begin writing my book *Pet Talker*, to be completed in the near future.

DEDICATION

This chapter is dedicated to my two dogs, Shooz and Midnite, who have passed on. These two taught me my animal communication abilities and because of them I have a different perspective on animals and their unconditional love. I love to share this information with others.

Unconditional Love

GEORGIA NAGEL

Native American legend says, "When a human dies, there is a bridge they must cross to enter into heaven. At the head of the bridge waits every animal that human encountered during their lifetime. The animals, based on what they know of this person, decide which humans may cross the bridge... and which are turned away."

It was ten years ago when I asked a medium/psychic I was working with what my life purpose was and she replied "to learn unconditional love." I have never forgotten those words and at first I thought she was talking about romantic love, which at that time was not looking good at all. In fact, I was living alone with my two dogs Shooz and Midnite, but was not lonely. My pet-sitting business was also starting to get really busy, so I had my animal clients. This consisted of dogs, cats, birds, chickens, ducks, geese, cattle, horses, ferrets, iguanas, fish, turtles and an African frog, all to keep me company. As I continued on with my life the words of the psychic were always in the back of my mind and I would often reflect on them. As my work with pet clients started opening me up more and more to their love, I noticed I was starting to let down the protective barrier I had placed around my heart without even knowing when in their company. Prior to this, I would go to a funeral and never shed a tear, but now if a client called and said they had to put their pet to sleep, I would be crying on the phone with them and sometimes days afterwards. What was happening? Could my heart be softening? Was I going through menopause? It didn't dawn on me at first that I was learning from the animals unconditional love; in fact, it would be a few years before I would figure it out.

Between my own two dogs and the pet clients I was working with, I began to realize that dogs especially had a love for their human families that a lot of people don't have for each other. Dogs have an unconditional love for their owners and they show it by their actions. I am not saying cats don't, but cats seem to choose when they want to give you love. When you walk in your house the dog is so excited to see you, even if they thought you should have been home hours ago. They understand when you are experiencing sorrow, sadness, and pain, and will sit right beside you and lick away your tears. They will listen to you as you complain about your day or anything else you want to share. The unconditional love of a pet is amazing and they have no problem giving it to others. Have you ever been to a nursing home when a volunteer brings in a pet for the elderly to visit with? The people are so excited they save treats for these pets and the dogs are so excited because they are getting their attention. If you watch the dogs, you'll see they don't care if a person has had a stroke and is unable to talk correctly; or their hands are shaking from Parkinson's disease; or they have dementia and can't remember the dog's name, and call him by a pet's name they had long ago when they were a child. A person does not have to be perfect to receive these animals' unconditional love.

I have watched children crawl all over the big family dog and it never flinches when they tug at its ears or tail. A friend's life was saved when her dog woke her with its persistent barking, and she got up to see her house was on fire. One of my clients has volunteered with her dog for Hospice over a span of five years. Her dog knows when it is time to go to work and waits for her vest to be put on and then they go to the patient's home or hospital room that is receiving Hospice. This dog will lie on their bed beside them as they pass away, if the family wishes. She brings peace and comfort to the patient and the family, all unconditionally. Many of my clients have pets they have rescued and they tell me they are the best pets they have ever owned. It is as if the pet is grateful to finally have a loving home where they can give love back.

This fall my friend and I are starting a program at our local animal shelter, where the younger students can come in and read to the cats. They will pick out a book and go into the cat room and read to the cats, a benefit to both the students and the cats. The students can practice their reading and nobody will judge them on how they read, while the cats can bond with the children. The students get volunteer hours and the cats get attention, a win-win situation for all involved. We will eventually expand that into reading with dogs. I have heard that children who volunteer in their community do better in school, learn to work with others and become self-motivators.

I truly believe that if we teach our younger generations to treat animals with respect and love they will benefit from it for the rest of their lives, as will the rest of the world. So many young people have not been taught how to treat animals respectfully. They think beating or kicking an animal is going to teach them right from wrong, but it only teaches them to run or fight back. I have read that a dog can have an I.Q. of a seven-year-old child, and that is quite intelligent. A client of mine is working with schools and going into the classroom to teach the students on how to care for an animal. These young kids are eager to learn and have all kinds of questions and sometimes tell how their animals are treated at home by their parents. That is when my client explains the correct way to care for an animal and answers their questions. I have also read that children who mistreat, abuse or torture animals when they are young can grow up to commit crimes, even murder.

I have known hard-hearted people who are miserable and have a stray cat or dog show up on their doorstep. They start to leave food out even as they grumble about it. Soon they are making a trip into town to buy dog or cat food, then the next trip is a dog or cat bed, then they are building a shelter for the yard or they let the animal into their house for a minute, which turns into half a day, then a whole day, and then permanently. Their whole life has changed; they become happier and have something to live for. Along the same lines, I have had clients who say they will never get another pet after their pet has died, it is too hard. Then one day an animal will show up at their house, they take it in and decide to care for it until they can find a home for it. That animal keeps chipping away at that broken heart, and the grief they had been suffering over the loss of their pet slowly disappears and they keep that animal, telling me it is the best thing that could have happened. I like to believe the animal found them when they needed love the most, to help with their grieving process.

In the past eighteen years of pet sitting I have noticed more sunrises and sunsets, and I have walked in the rain and enjoyed it, as the dogs and I splash through mud puddles. I have learned to appreciate those times when a dog stops to look at something crawling across the ground, whether it's a spider, beetle, frog or snake. The last one makes a little harder for me to stand still and watch. When the dogs stop and put their noses in the air, what is it that they smell? Is it flowers or an upcoming rainstorm? Or maybe it is the scent of another animal or somebody grilling outside. If we are walking along and they stand perfectly still, not a muscle moving, I know they have spotted something ahead that I might not see, so I try to determine what it is that has their attention. I have been in a yard of beautiful lush grass and the dogs have rolled around on it, and I am not ashamed to say I have joined them. What a wonderful way to ground yourself with mother earth. At night when walking with them I have heard owls hooting, frogs croaking, seen falling stars and full moons, and noted the peacefulness of the night. I have enjoyed watching kittens play;

cats chase flies around the house or pounce at them on window panes. I truly enjoy playing hide and seek with cats and dogs; they always find me and that makes them so happy, but at the same time they must be thinking, it is not too difficult finding you but we will play along. I have had rotten days and arrive at a house where the dog will sit beside me and lick my face as if to say it's ok, I love you; or a kitten or puppy will make me laugh with their silly antics. They teach you love, the unconditional kind, forever and ever, loyal through ups and downs, bad times or good, as long as they can be at your side. From a young age to the end of their lives, they have so much to teach us if we would just open our hearts and take the time to learn from them. There is a saying I like, "If I could only be the person my pet thinks I am." If we would take half of the love that animals give and apply it to others in our lives, allow it to change how we treat others, it would be a much better world.

There is a poem I read often and try to apply not only to animals but also to humans, because the animal part comes easily to me, and I am still working on the "unconditional love" the psychic told me about so many years ago.

THE RESCUERS QUILT

As I arrived at the Bridge, I faced all the animals that had gone before me.

Before each of us go to the Bridge, we live our lives like the squares of a quilt, mirrored in the eyes of the animals awaiting us. An animal Angel sits before each of us sewing our quilt squares together in a tapestry that is our life. But as my Angel took each piece of cloth off the pile, I noticed how ragged and empty each of my squares was.

They were filled with giant holes. Each square was labeled with a part of my life as a rescuer that had been difficult, the challenges I was faced with in my quest to save lives, and the times I had been tempted to take the easy way out and avoid the controversy rather than speak for the animal that could not speak for itself.

I saw hardships that I had endured for the sake of the animals, which were the largest holes of all. I glanced around me. Nobody else had such squares. Other than a tiny hole here and there, the other tapestries were filled with rich color and the bright hues of worldly fortune. I gazed upon my own life and was disheartened. My animal Angel was sewing the ragged pieces together, threadbare and empty, like binding air.

Finally, the time came when each life was to be displayed, held up to the light, to the scrutiny of truth. The others rose; each in turn, holding up their tapestries. So filled their lives had been with the riches of the Earth. My animal Angel looked upon me, and nodded for me to rise. My gaze dropped to the ground in shame. I hadn't had all the earthly fortunes. I had love in my life, and laughter and the sweet kisses of the precious animals that had honored my life with their presence. But there had also been the trials of illness, and death, and false accusations that took me from the world as I knew it. I had to start over many times. I often struggled with the temptation to quit, only to somehow muster the strength to pick up and begin again. I spent many nights crying and praying that somehow the strength would come to go on, asking for help and guidance as I tried to help the helpless. I had often been held up to ridicule, which I endured painfully, each time accepting it for the sake of the animals that looked at me with trust and love in their eyes.

And now I had to face the truth. My life was what it was, and I had to acknowledge it. I rose and slowly lifted the combined squares of my life to the light. An awe-filled gasp filled the air. I gazed around at the animals gathered there, who stared at me with wide eyes. Then, I looked upon the tapestry before me.

Light flooded the many holes, creating an image of an animal that had depended on me. All the animals at the Bridge stood before me, with warmth and love in their eyes. They said, "Every time you gave your life to help us, it gave us life. Each point of light in your life is when you stepped aside to let us shine through, until there was more of us than there was of you'

May all our quilts be threadbare and worn, allowing the animals to shine through.

~Unknown

If we all can take a little time to appreciate the other inhabitants we share this world with and show them and ourselves some kindness and unconditional love, like the kind you receive from a pet, this earth just might be a little more peaceful.

CHAPTER Seventeen

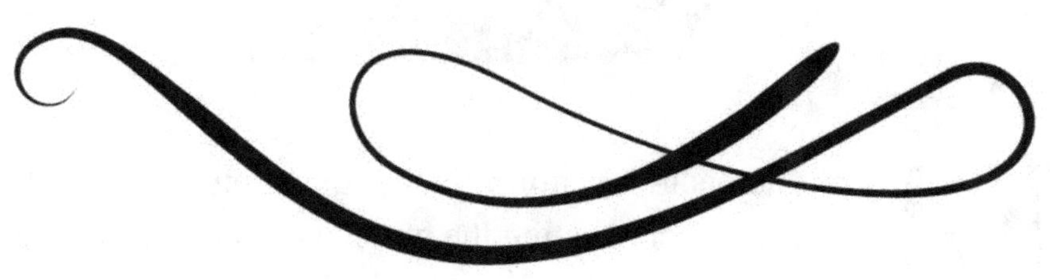

Peace and Health Go Hand in Hand

TIFFANY JOHNSON

My mission is to transform lives. I'm an intuitive adjuster and healer reconnecting the mind and body. I give hope and instill the belief that your body can heal and your life can change. We are not broken, but whole, and I help put the pieces of the puzzle back together. Anything is possible if you believe—in yourself, in your body and in the power within you to change your life.

Besides running a high-volume pediatric/family practice, I am a wife of 16 years and a mom of a 15-year-old girl and 12-year-old boy. I love my kitties, building memories with family, reading, writing, snuggling, connecting with close friends, music and sports (both cheering and coaching).

My motto is: *Life isn't always easy, but it's worth pursuing its gifts. Once you decide that you* ***deserve*** *to have it all, you can; and when you* ***allow*** *it to come to you, it will.*

Watch for my new book coming out early 2017, "From Last Resort to First Option: How Chiropractic Will Change Your Life."

Contact:

www.htchiro.com

drtiffany@htchiro.com

Facebook: Healing Touch Chiropractic

ACKNOWLEDGEMENT

To Craig, my life partner, anchor (when I'm flying in the clouds) and hot air balloon (when I doubt I can fly): You knew my gift far before I trusted it.

To Callyn and Gavin, our lights to the world: You are strong, confident and driven to make an impact.

And finally, to my team, oh, my goodness, my team: You have cleared every path I have trail-blazed.

DEDICATION

Sophia, Richard, Sarah and Tate, your willingness to share your story, to be persistent in seeking a miracle, and the gut check to follow your heart will help millions find hope and allow many to witness a miracle through Chiropractic.

Peace and Health Go Hand in Hand

DR. TIFFANY JOHNSON

My Mission: *To Transform Lives. Anything is possible if you believe…in yourself, your body, and the power within you to heal.*

Let's get real: Our families are sick, our communities are sick and our world is sick. We may wonder how we as individuals can make a difference. As Gandhi said, "Be the change you wish to see in the world." This one statement is world-renown as it speaks to the reflection of oneself. Don't worry about what others are saying, doing and thinking; instead, look within and be that change. Without transformational health, we have nothing.

The definition of Peace is freedom from disturbance; quiet and tranquility; mental calm and serenity. Contrary to that, when your mind, body and soul are in a state of noise, agitation and inner conflict, this will lead to dis-ease. Eventually our body may become stressed enough that we get the bad news, the news that while some have time to change their mindset and lifestyle, unfortunately, some don't. In working with thousands of grandmas, grandpas, moms, dads and their kids, I've found there is no greater stress than lack of health. And no greater peace than health.

Kids believe what they see and hear starting at a young age. This is where "Common vs. Normal" comes in. Here are some examples:

- If they grew up watching their mom struggle with depression and anxiety and the only thing that took the physical and emotional pain away is a little pill = Normal.
- If they grew up watching their dad always take Advil when he had neck and back pain = Normal.
- If they grew up watching their parent needing to sleep in a dark, quiet room while taking the rest of the workday off, consuming a pill/receiving a shot/visiting the ER when they get a headache or migraine = Normal.
- If they grew up using an inhaler every time it was difficult to breathe = Normal.
- If they grew up with their sister eating prunes or taking Miralax every time she couldn't eliminate = Normal.
- If they grew up with their grandparents taking Claritin every spring and fall because of "allergies" = Normal.

But is it really normal?

Anxiety, depression, chronic pain, headaches, migraines, asthma, constipation and allergies are NOT normal. For the majority of families, though, these complaints are so frequently experienced and/or heard that they become household norms. I see this every day in my practice. Statements like, "Little Janey (at 6), is really healthy so at least I don't have to worry about her." When we dig further, I find out that Little Janey had a rough birth, multiple ear infections in her first year, gets sick 1-2x/year with the common cold and has mild spring and fall allergies. She has been on about five antibiotics in her short life and takes cold medicine and Claritin when needed. When we compare the unhealthy to the unhealth-ier, we are comparing average to below average. Or maybe you're comparing your 'healthy child' with your best friend's child who is chronically sick (on antibiotics, medications and struggles every day with numerous issues). Why don't you strive for great health? Why are those things listed above considered “normal”?

Imagine if…your child has never been medicated, never taken to the doctor, or never had any acute or chronic issues? Imagine if…your teenager has never struggled with anxiety, depression, headaches, PMS, or stomach issues. Do you think this is possible?

YES! I’ve lived it personally with my kids, and have mentored and adjusted thousands of other kids to live this life. It is possible. Sophia is one example of a MIRACLE when the body and mind is given what it needs to heal.

A few years ago and a month before her 4th birthday, I met Sophia’s family. It was their last-ditch effort to change their daughter’s life through Chiropractic. Those first few days of conversations were heartbreaking. Comments like, “Her brother thinks she’s going to die,” and “I don’t know if our family can withstand this stress,” and “Our next step is brain surgery,” ripped my heart in half yet in the next breath, it gave me even more purpose, more passion and more hope to get this girl well. I knew the ramifications—it was life or death for this family and I was going to be the one to help bring her back to life through Chiropractic.

This is where Sophia’s journey started:

At the age of 2, she had her first seizure and stroke. Her body shut down. They went on a journey to learn of other diagnoses like anxiety, insomnia, ASD, ADD, ADHD, ODD, SPD, and OCD. She never slept more than 2 hours/day so one parent was up with her around the clock. She stopped walking, talking and eating solid foods. She wasn’t able to be in small or large groups anymore so they were bound to their apartment. She harmed herself and others.

Their days were chock-full of appointments, up to 30 hours every week between numerous pediatricians, neurologists and therapists…still with no answers or changes. Shortly after her diagnosis, she started on a cocktail of medication, creating more side effects, and eventually she was taking 1000mg of an adult sedative (the average adult is on 50mg) with no changes. The next step was brain surgery.

Then the referral to Mayo in Rochester opened up doors. These doctors were receptive to natural options and the hope that eventually Sophia could live a life with no medications, surgeries or limitations. They believed there was another option, one better than the life she had been living for 2 years. That brought the family into my office—and what followed was the first glimmer of hope and support, and the search for a miracle.

That day in the office was a tearjerker for all of us. After they shared her story, I proceeded with the exam and nerve scan. It was very clear there was a disruption in her upper neck, at the level of the brainstem. Her body was stuck in a fight/flight state and her nervous system was in overdrive. Think of it like this: Back in the day, when a boy wanted to show-off and get your attention in his truck, he would rev the gas (ha, did that bring you back to the good ol' days?!). Humor aside, that was the state that Sophia's brain and body were in 100% of the time. Revved and in overdrive.

After her first Adjustment, she fell asleep on the drive home. (Remember that she hadn't slept for over 2 hours at a time since she was 2 years old). That day, they could instantly tell the change in her behavior, patience, interaction and sleep patterns. Over the next 6 months, this is how her life transformed, and what it is today:

- Seizure and stroke free
- Medication free
- Diagnosis free
- Therapy free
- Can walk, talk and eat solid foods

- Able to play and interact with others
- Sleeps 8-12 hours a night
- Started Kindergarten!

You may be wondering how Chiropractic changed her life. The precursor to the adjustment was faith, hope and a deep commitment on the part of Sophia's parents that they were willing to do whatever it takes. The adjustment was magic…it rebalanced and reconnected her brain and body. It turned the circuit breaker switch back on. It took the kink out of the garden hose. All of this, to restore health and life in this little girl's brain and body.

Without the *hope* and *persistence* of her parents, Sophia wouldn't be who she is today. And this, my friends, has provided Peace in their family and for everyone who knows and loves them. Instead of living in fear, they live in gratitude for their life and are compassionate to others who are also experiencing difficult situations.

As Sarah said, "Instead of Chiropractic being the last resort, make it your first option."

This is just one story, one miracle, yet look at the ripple effect…

What is your story of health? Or your child's story? If I could wave a magic wand over your health, what three things would you want changed (or improved)?

1.______________________________

2.______________________________

3.______________________________

Next, circle the one that will have the most impact on your life and tackle that first (and do the same with each member of your family). As soon as you decide and feel the change in your heart, you will achieve it. Peace, just like health, is an "inside job." And it starts with YOU. Be a role model of health in mind, body and spirit. Take full responsibility (that means no excuses), and be accountable to something greater than yourself. We all have the power to create the ripple effect. It only starts with one, YOU.

Here are the ABC's of adding more peace to your life:

1. **A**ccept the compliment, accept the gift. People want to take care of you.
2. **B**e grateful for everything in your life.
3. **C**an't is a swear word. Eliminate these words from your vocabulary: can't, won't, shouldn't, never, have to, need to.

Now, about your kids…their level of peace and health start with you, too! I know, I know, you may be rolling your eyes by now. But for real, they are watching you. Strive not to be perfect, but kind. Strive not to be a follower, but a leader. Strive to use your voice so they learn to use theirs.

From working with thousands of kids and their parents in private practice, this is what I hope we as parents will spend more time teaching:

- How the body works and we were born with everything it needs to heal
- That every physical complaint is intertwined with an emotion
- That every choice they make moves them towards or away from health
- That the body is created perfectly, without pills, potions or lotions
- That what we put into the body has the direct result of what comes out
- That listening to that gut instinct will never lead you astray

Understanding these truths in our lives will assist you in leading your children to be awake, aware and healthy. Let go of the "woulda, coulda, shoulda" stuff and start now by wiping your slate clean. As Buddha says, "There are only two mistakes one can make along the road to truth; not going all the way, and not starting."

Sophia's story [1]is a testimony to how one person's miracle can change the world, give hope and offer peace within families. Step up to make a difference in your world and in the life of everyone who looks up to you. You will make a ripple that the world needs.

[1] http://htchiro.com/seizures-and-chiropractic-a-forever-changed-family/

CHAPTER *Eighteen*

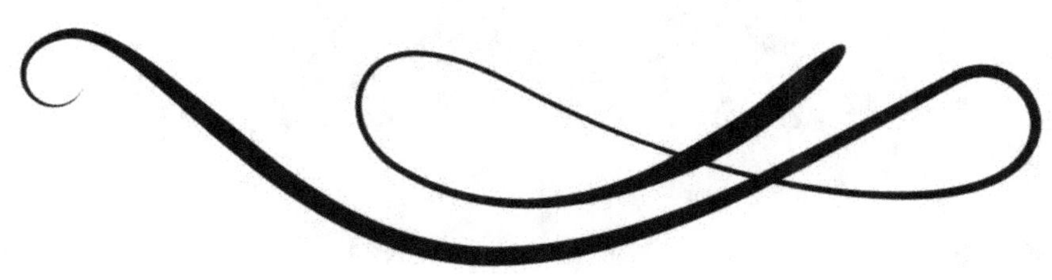

The Church of Kindness

BARBARA E. HARRIS

Barbara "Bobbi" Harris was a Real Estate Broker and Appraiser when she was called back into nursing by a life-changing event. She had a Near Death Experience (NDE) in 1983, which she writes of in *Conversations with Mary: Modern Miracles in an Everyday Life*. Reviews describe the book as "infused with the lyricism of a mystical poet," and as having "mystical accounts of direct, intimate union with the Divine…"

Her nursing career would evolve over the next three decades culminating in the coveted certification as a Holistic Nurse. Bobbi has earned B.A. and M.S. degrees as well.

During her writing career, Bobbi has also penned many poems. She recently joined the Spiritual Writer's Association and has been published in the poetry anthologies, *Finding Our Wings: A Collection of Angelic Short Stories and Poem, 2015* and *The Light Within: A Collection of Peace and Prose, 2016.*

Barbara resides in Sarasota, Florida.

ACKNOWLEDGEMENTS

I wish to give special thanks to R.D. Petti, my friend and fellow Spiritual author, who has supported me during the last year after the passing of my beloved husband. Without her encouragement to join The Spiritual Writer's Network and her invitation to become a part of this wonderful book project, I would not be writing. Her steadfast calm during my struggle with computer crashes is something I will always treasure.

I also want to thank Shanda Trofe for giving authors and poets who are spiritual a home where they can express themselves and have their work recognized. It truly is a Spiritual Endeavor!

DEDICATION

I wish to thank my late husband, Rev. Dr. Linton I. "Chip" Harris, who made his transition on September 26, 2015. His forty years of unconditional love, belief and encouragement in me as a writer gave me the courage to compose both stories and poetry. Without his guidance and patience with me on the computer none of this would have manifested. He will always be in my heart.

The Church of Kindness

BARBARA E. HARRIS

Make Gentle the Earth

Come on, women, gather round.
This time it's us who'll make the sound.
Make gentle the earth; make lovely the sky.
To this, Lord, now listen, a woman's cry.
Peace we write, Peace we pray.
Never has there been a day
Since we were born that did not see
Babies torn and ravished be.
Oh God, who dwells in grey-hued sky,
Hear us when our souls do cry.

The images on the television were so upsetting and offensive that I stopped watching the news. It is heart-wrenching to watch urban violence and the suffering of millions of people around the globe. What influence can one person have on this chaos? How can we help achieve peace among all nations? I have learned one thing in this lifetime…change must begin with me. But what could I do? Months of meditation on my intention of attaining peace produced the same answer: "Start a church." It was a preposterous message! No matter how many times I meditated, expecting another answer, it was always the same. The message, though clear as a bell, was not workable for me.

At that time, I was the sole caretaker of my wonderful husband of forty years, who had Pick's Disease, a form of dementia. We had promised each other not to make use of institutions at the end of our lives. I fulfilled that pledge for over two years. Included in this was the formidable task of packing up and moving from our large home to a smaller home in a lovely gated, maintenance-free community.

It was during this period that the Boston Marathon bombing happened. It hit very close to home. My twin brother, his wife, and their two married daughters lived in the Boston suburbs. Some of them were on the parade route that day. My niece, her husband and three children had left the spot at the finish line where a bomb was detonated because their friend finished the race fifteen minutes earlier. Needless to say, I was shaken to my very core. It could have been one of them who was injured, maimed or killed. The thought of the little boy Martin who was injured and later died moved me to tears, and it was then when this poem was born.

Senseless Violence

First there was Martin, then Bobby and Jack.
Our souls were torn; our hearts did wrack.
Once again we view carnage and strife,
Though this time they took a younger life.
Another Martin suffering the same fate,
Though this angel messenger was only eight.
"Peace," he said, "don't hurt people anymore."
When will we learn the message he bore?
Oh, God who dwells in heavenly skies,
Listen, please listen, to our cries.
Our eyes grow dim, our souls are numb.
Please Lord, touch the hearts of everyone.

Surely now I must do something. One evening when I was in prayer and meditation, a light bulb went off in my head. I did not need a building to start a church! I would be the founder of the Church of Kindness. This church would be headquartered in my HEART! Anyone could join, requiring no donations, no meetings, no services, no choir, and no minister. Once your heart was pledged to this church, you would promise to be kind to all people you met, as well as all of God's other creatures. You also pledged to donate a financial gift weekly to someone of your choice.

I affirmed that this church would officially open on the date of my husband's transition and my mother's birthday, September 26, 2015. My husband had served for many hours in service to hospitals, nursing homes, and hospices. In his lifetime he exemplified the art of kindness.

Soon the day came when my husband made his transition. Sadly, I now had all the time in the world to practice the tenet of the Church of Kindness. I noted that many of my close friends and family members did not attend church. However, these people were compassionate individuals; many were employed in assistance professions, and all were practicing kindness, in endeavors from rescuing dogs and protecting turtle nests to feeding the homeless and mentoring children.

Many would ask me, "Where do you go to church?" I could not wait to answer, "I go to the Church of Kindness!" The next question was always, "Where is that church?" and I could gleefully answer, "It's in my heart!" Often, in these encounters, I found that people looked perplexed for a moment and then started to smile. The answer always opened up a lively conversation.

I explained that the church had a "collection plate" that involved giving to others weekly. Members must pledge to perform an act of kindness each week that involved a donation to the "collection plate." This "plate" existed anywhere they chose to give a financial donation. It could be as simple as enlarging a tip for a waiter or waitress whose service was outstanding. I also gave those that asked one word of caution; they would experience more joy than the recipient of their kindness.

I went out of my way to be kind to others and to look for ways to put my weekly donation in the "plate." My grief and empty hours spurred me on. What I noticed was there were so many opportunities to be kind to others. One of my favorite and most-fun donations to the "plate" is to go through a fast food restaurant drive-in and give the boy or girl behind the window a twenty dollar bill, or perhaps less, depending on what my expenses that week allowed. One young African-American youngster of about sixteen years of age shouted, "Hey everybody! The lady in the blue car gave me this!" and he waved the bill excitedly over his head. He then called out from the window at me, "Thank you, lady. Now I can buy some shoes!" My happiness was mixed with sorrow when I thought of how many pairs of shoes I had in my closet.

Although my actions of giving to the "plate" for the Church of Kindness are too numerous to list, there are a few that have left an indelible impression on my mind and heart. One stands out above all others and inspired this poem.

A Goodbye Gift

I looked up and saw him in the chair.
Astounded…I watched her take off his hair.
Something stirred in my heart that day,
Then for him I started to pray.
He looked like a soldier going to war,
His hair, he would not need anymore.
How I hoped it was not the case,
As I sent him Love filled with Grace.
Then I decided for the haircut to pay;

My giving to the plate for that day.
Whisking off the cape, showing his clothes,
Sure enough… fatigues and boots over hose.
He would defend our country soon.
My heart skipped a beat for his platoon.
He was going to a land of killing and strife,
For us… this lad would risk his life.
Tears flooded my eyes as he left,
I have seldom felt so bereft.
Pleading fervently to God in prayer,
Bring PEACE to all everywhere.

I continued to watch from afar as he mouthed the word "WHO?" I felt so much joy. Of course, the beautician was silent. He stood up and gave a loud "Whoop!" and walked over to a young woman. Giving her a hug, he suddenly shouted out, "Hey! Now we can go for pizza!" The beautician told me later that this young man was about to ship out for combat in Afghanistan. The young woman was his bride. Again, my joy was mixed with sorrow as I thought of him going to war. I felt so sad to see them walk away.

I was now noticing opportunities everywhere to be kind. Just a smile to a stranger and a "Hi!" lit up people's faces. One day I stopped my car alongside the road to pick up a woman walking while carrying two gallon jugs of water. It was August in Florida and the heat and humidity were intense. "Wow! What a great town this is!" she exclaimed, while climbing into my air-conditioned car. "This is my first day living here and my water is not turned on yet. My landlord brought me dinner and a bag of food!" she said with enthusiasm. "What church do you attend, maybe I can go there?" was her first question to me. Ah! Now the fun began. She wanted to go to my church! So then I said the words I loved the most…ending with "it's in my heart." The best part is observing the facial expressions that accompany my answer. Her expression was initially one of confusion that ended with grinning and laughter. Then she said, "What a great idea! I am going to tell the people I meet about it." Driving away, I reflected on how before my awareness was raised, I would have just sped on by. I would have been in too great a hurry to notice her. If that one act could make such a difference in a person's life, what could be accomplished if we all began thinking this way? I began to increase my awareness, not only of what I could do, but what others might do, as well.

One day my daughter-in-law, Sharon, called and told me about an occurrence that morning in Oregon. It exemplified a spirit of Love and Kindness that embodied the philosophy of this new Church. I was so touched that this poem came spilling out.

Love Expressed

'Twas a frosty view that early morn,
When through the window I saw torn
A hummingbird, from a nearby tree.
Now silent, with wings stilled, was she.

Bumped by another from the perch,
She had fallen with a jolting lurch.
Dazed and startled, not moving now.
I need to save her! But knew not how.

I knew my heart would show the way,
That icy, grey, December day.
Without thinking, action I took
Before she was in an animal's hook.

Picking her up gently with my hand,
I removed her from the frosty land.
Wrapped her in a cloth warm and soft,
And placed her in a box on my loft.

While preparing her food I did hear
The sound of wings fluttering near.
I raised the window; she left in a flash,
Joined Mother Nature from my window sash.

Looking at her I knew she was fine.
Gazing back at me, her eyes did shine.
I think that I shall never see
A lovelier, innocent expression of Thee.

This is kindness…no one was watching…yet a soul was stirred by the plight of the newborn hummingbird. This is but an example of the philosophy behind the Church of Kindness. Kindness can work for everyone. It is possible for all of us who consider ourselves as belonging to the human family.

In his book, *Rhythms of Vision: The Changing Patterns of Belief,* author Lawrence Blair PhD discusses the Hundredth Monkey Phenomenon. It tells of Japanese scientists observing monkeys living on an island. They were given sweet potatoes covered with sand. One day a young monkey took the sweet potato to a stream and dipped it in the water before eating it. Soon, all the monkeys on the island began to do the same. What scientists could not explain was how the cleansing of the sweet potato jumped across the sea onto other islands. Quantum physics explains that when a critical mass achieves an awareness, it may be communicated from mind to mind. We are all connected…we are all one. It is therefore possible that the Church of Kindness can spread throughout the world, one heart at a time. It is often the simplest of acts that have the most impact.

"Peace is not something you wish for; it's something you MAKE, something you DO, something you ARE, and something YOU GIVE AWAY."
~John Lennon

CHAPTER Nineteen

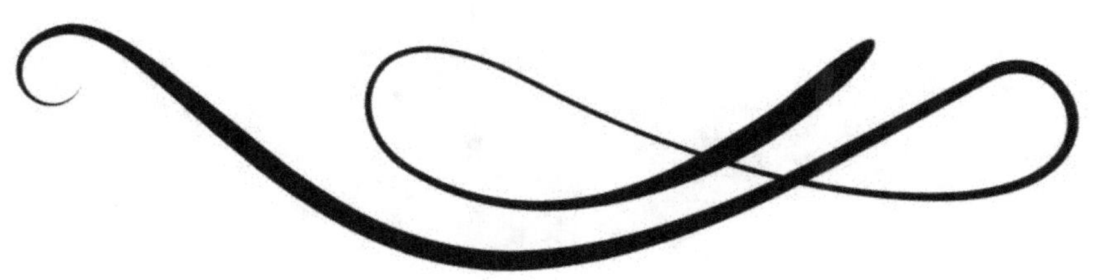

Little Eagle

KATRINA ELKINS

Katrina Elkins, author and a certified Breath of Love facilitator, is cultivating a new awareness of the power of self-love, community, and the true meaning of healing from old traumas.

Having overcome a childhood lived in a fear-based, apocalyptic cult Katrina awakens us to the beauty of life in the present moment. She invites us to live fiercely and relish the richness of being open to our effortless abundance. She invites the reader to see the unending joy that comes with the power of play our inner child craves, and celebrates.

Katrina speaks of the ease and grace available to all, both men and women, from the Divine Feminine. Her writings show fearlessness in following the soul's quest of discovering its true and boundless potential. She teaches that peace ignites from within and we are to greet it with love and compassion. Ultimately, we are meant to live connected and in alignment with the gifts and bounty of the Universe.

Connect with Katrina

Email:

Info@katrinaelkins.com

Website

www.katrinaelkins.com

Facebook

www.facebook.com/katrinaelkins

ACKNOWLEDGEMENTS

I have had many great teachers who have passed on to the next part of their journey. My husband and young two children have opened a new world of amazement around me, as well as given me a renewed trust in God. They have shown me the support I needed as I followed my dreams. Shanda Trofe and Julia Mikk have been fundamental in helping me realize the importance of mentors and the role they play in expanding my horizons and in finding the value of community.

DEDICATION

I am grateful for the vulnerability of my readers, who are willing to explore what it means to be a human walking and breathing on this intense, wild, and extraordinary planet. Thank you.

Little Eagle

KATRINA ELKINS

Little Eagle,
She has shown me
The river that flows with ease and grace.

She has shown me
Love and peace.
She is Little Eagle,
Born only a year ago.

Her toes dance
Lightly and effortlessly
Along the dusty path.

Exuberant joy extends
From her heart
As she dances among
The Feminine.

Little Eagle soars
With her hands
Touching the celestial;
Bodies of light surround her.

Her legs yearn to know
The dance of life
On this blessed and abundant Mother
We call our home.

Her glory is not in following.
Her radiance is simply in BEING.
There are no rules to
lock her
In mistrust and fear.

With unending support
From the Divine Feminine,
Her leaps and twirls
awaken my own inner child.

The child who never forgot
That she is enough.
The child of golden
Light that yearns to dance
With the Divine.

She beacons me out
Onto the stage.
The stage with her mothers and aunts
And grandmothers.

I have been bound by the rules
In my own heart;
Disconnected from the Source of joy.

Her unending fervor
Is the fire that ignites
My own desire to
Dance freely and blissfully.

My ancestors are with her ancestors.
My life is part of her life.

We are one.
We are connected.
She has shown me
That I am complete.

One exuberant step
Allows the next, taken by
Her legs that yearned to touch the earth.

She is part of the river of the
Divine Mother.
Her dance is glorious,
Little Eagle's.

I go to the Divine Feminine now
In this time of tremendous growth,
And call for unending trust within.

Little Eagle shows me the
Grounding love of Mother Earth,
And the freedom to soar with the
Heights of Divine energy.
She giggles and her
Countenance lights up as
She opens the gates for the
Tears shed from her ancestors.

A new path
Has been forged
For all those tears
That were shed.

For my ancestors and her ancestors,
A new world of understanding and love
Has arrived today.

The wings of Little Eagle are expansive
And filled with the feathers of a million dreams.

She is a healer.
She is a leader.

She is the way of
The river that
Flows freely.

She is the lightness in
The breeze that touches my
Brow and tickles my senses.
Ethereal, mystical,
Magical, mesmerizing.

She shows me the
Way that I have always known
But have not trusted
Within the old manmade structures.

Let the dam of
My perceived
Fears burst
And welcome the
Unending nourishment
Of the Divine Feminine.

The Earthly structures are crumbling.
She is demonstrating
Love from the Divine Feminine.

She is love. She is Little Eagle.

She helps me to trust new structures
That will support her celestial bounty
In the freedom of her dance.

The unraveling has begun.
I have received news of her arrival
With visions and whispers
Floating on the wind.

Her twirls, with arms outstretched,
Lift the black cape
That adorns her small body,
Demonstrating her glee.

A joy that floats through the passage
Of all time and space.

An unfolding era has come
That accompanies
All aspects of
DIVINE presence
And BEING.

She is the joy
In my daughter's
smile. She is the
Energy of my
Earthly Mother.

Little EAGLE
Is calling me forward
To commune and dance
With arms spread wide
And feet rooted to

The depths of the
Mother Earth.

She has welcomed
Me onto the stage of Life.

My ancestors are her ancestors.
The dance has begun,
And now it is time to release
The hold on our hearts.

The peace we all
Desire is here, right now,
Calling forth my inner child
to play.

My wings will soar with her.
My heart will soar with her.
I will surrender to the Divine urge
To play and dance. Will you?

CHAPTER *Twenty*

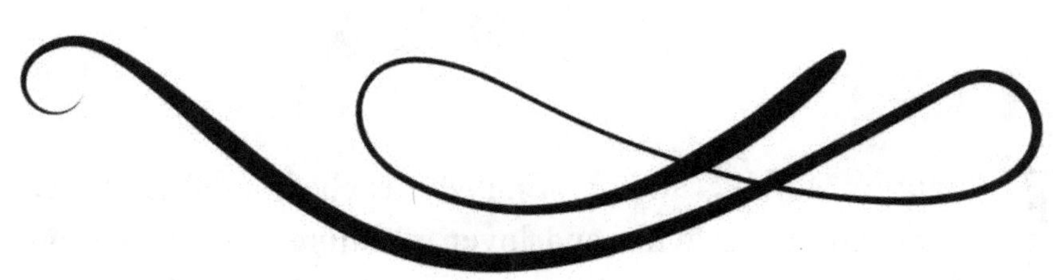

Unconditional Kindness

LAURIE MOLLOY

Laurie Molloy, author; English teacher; mother of two amazing boys; wife; and lover of nature, poetry, learning, walking, swimming, people, and the light and goodness she sees in the world. She is the founder of Borrowed Books, LLC, a small business with the mission, "Less scrolling screens, more flipping pages." She is often found at the park, pool, or posting on Google Plus, Blogger, WordPress, and her own Facebook discussion forum, also named Borrowed Books.

Laurie has loved writing since middle school. In eighth grade, she won a writing contest for an essay on *The Time Machine* by H.G. Wells. She recently collaborated on a haiku and photography book with a friend that won a publication award and will be printed soon.

Laurie's children and students inspire her to be kinder, more compassionate, and to always endeavor to become more enlightened. Through teaching and listening, she continues to learn and is driven to develop new ways to inspire the passions of those around her.

Link up with Laurie

Email: lauriemolloy25@gmail.com

Websites

www.lauriemolloy.com

https://lauriemolloy.wordpress.com/

https://laurie-molloy.blogspot.com/

Social Media

https://www.facebook.com/laurie.molloy1

https://plus.google.com/u/0/+LaurieMolloy

ACKNOWLEDGEMENT

I am thankful to my parents, who raised me to believe in peace and justice; my husband, who encourages me to strive to be my best; and Linda (Reiki Teacher), who has elevated my awareness to a new level that, before completing her courses, I am not sure I could have attained.

DEDICATION

This chapter is dedicated to Lynn La Rocco and Ann and Greg Ziffer; their sincerity and love are surely welcome in the world. I would also like to thank Melissa Corter and Shanda Trofe, who set into motion the actualization of my first book.

Unconditional Kindness

LAURIE MOLLOY

Interview with Lynn LaRocco:
A Story of Unconditional Kindness and Love

I had the pleasure of meeting Lynn in person after becoming acquainted with her on Facebook. The generosity of her neighbors, Ann and Greg Ziffer, allowed her to see there was a world waiting for her outside her own experience; a world with light, kindness, and opportunity.

Lynn's neighbors and friends were essential to her life. A few years after Lynn's father passed away, Lynn's mother began dating a man named Randy. Eventually, Lynn's mother sold their family home and moved herself, Lynn, and Lynn's little brother into Randy's home.

Her mom and stepfather did not set rules or boundaries, and Lynn was left to live life by her own rules. By the time Lynn was sixteen she was working full-time while attending high school. As a senior, Lynn had her own apartment.

Lynn's family had always been close with the Ziffer family. After Lynn's dad passed, they took Lynn in when she needed a place to go. They accepted and guided her, giving her an escape from her tumultuous upbringing.

Here is Lynn's story, in her words… (portions of her story have been edited)

I grew up in a seemingly normal family. My mom and dad were very much in love, always hugging, and dancing in the house;

smitten. My father was a chef and my mom bounced around between menial jobs and periods home with us. They did not have much, but they never allowed us children to know that. My dad was the life of the party. He was funny, witty, and charismatic; someone everyone looked forward to seeing.

Every day my older brother Garrett and I played outside with the neighborhood kids, it did not matter the season. In the winter we built a sledding track down a hill or climbed trees to pretend we lived high in the "snow village." In the spring and summer months we played kickball and hockey in the street. We freely roamed the neighborhood from home to home, where all of the neighborhood parents made us feel welcome. It was not until I was an adult that I realized how truly blessed we were to be part of the last generation of kids able to safely play in the streets.

Our family was always close with our neighbors, Anne and Greg. They had two children, Carolyn and Chris, who were the same ages as Garrett and me. Their lives were always structured, and their children were given chores that they always performed. Carolyn, Chris, Garrett and I were all drawn to each other; we had an inseparable bond.

On June 30, 1991 my life as I knew it was gone, in the blink of an eye. I was seven years old and our phone rang; I could tell by the look on my mom's face that something was seriously wrong. My father had been in a car accident. She called Ann and Greg and another neighbor. Both families' husbands drove my mother two hours away to sit with her at the hospital and hold her hand as she heard the news: My father was deceased upon the arrival of his medivac helicopter. When I returned home the next afternoon with my neighbor, we found my mom sitting in the dark with the blinds drawn, lights off. Before she could say anything, I knew that my life had changed forever. Even at seven, sometimes you just know. My father was never coming home.

My father was only 36 years old. He had no life insurance, retirement money, nothing. My mom borrowed money while we waited out litigation (for four years) with the person who sideswiped my father's vehicle. After paying her debts and putting a small amount aside for my brother and me, my mother was left with $30,000 to raise two children and pay a mortgage.

During that same time period my future stepfather, Randy, was going through a wicked divorce. His wife had cheated while he thought she was seeing a marriage counselor. When this came to light, she left, leaving him with three boys and a soon-to-be serious drinking problem. He had always been a partier but he took it to another level, where it remained for the next 20 years.

Two years passed and my mom began dating. When we discovered she was dating Randy, we freaked. Randy's boys were unruly, and Randy himself was a drunk. It was not long until Mom packed us up and moved us all into Randy's home with his boys. Luckily I was given my own room without having to share with the now four boys in the house. My room was 9x8, had no closet, and was my paradise from what was going on outside those four walls.

It did not take long for my mom to start drinking. This was not the mother I knew, but this was the "new mom." That was the worst part; knowing who she was before and seeing what she had become. It was awful, a train wreck that I wanted to stop but could not. I had no voice. Though I would speak my mind at a young age, no one was listening to a near ten-year-old.

I spent as much time away from the house as I could with any friend that would take me. My go-to retreat was Anne and Greg's home; I did not have to pretend when I was there. They always had a place set at the table for me, and a spare mattress or sleeping bag so I could sleepover. They knew what I was going home to and they chose to allow me a better environment. The Ziffers took me school shopping, on vacations, and sightseeing.

Back home on weeknights it was the usual party scene: my parents inviting home stray "new friends" from the bar to continue drinking into the early morning hours despite our having to be up early for school. On weekends we would go on the boat from 10am until 11pm with coolers of beer, tied up with friend's boats while everyone partied, surrounded by adolescent children. We would be tired and cold and were told we could lie down in the back of the boat with a towel until we went home. My parents still recall these as "fun memories," but for us it was not fun at all. It was uncomfortable and unpleasant but no one cared. We had no voice.

As the years passed, we went on outings less and the party was contained to our home. Our house was always full of my parents' friends on school nights. At 9pm dinnertime, my stepfather was so intoxicated his face was three inches away from his plate while he grunted at his dinner. I observed this in utter disgust while my mom pretended to laugh, but I know on the inside she was not enjoying it. If he did not go to sleep promptly after dinner the real fun began. Randy would get argumentative and we would get defensive; arguments would start and Randy would butt my brother into a corner, push him against the wall, and take his door off the hinges so he couldn't slam his door to get away. With Randy it was never enough, he would keep coming out of his bedroom for more and my mom would just watch. She knew his behavior was not right, and I realize now that she allowed this treatment of us because outside of this, she had nothing. She had given up our home and spent any money she had. She was trapped and so were we.

More and more I retreated to the Ziffers' home because I felt understood and normal there. They never asked questions. They knew what my new life was and they never turned me away. I was much different than their daughter who was poised, smart and reserved. I was wearing short shorts, acting inappropriate at times and maybe not always the best influence. Regardless, they still accepted me, probably because they knew the reasons behind my poor choices.

Staying with the Ziffers for days was a breath of fresh air. My anxiety would leave; I could watch a movie with a family, bake Christmas cookies and participate in a normal life. At around 13 years old, I realized that my mother CHOSE her new life but I did not have to choose to be part of it. I spent a year living at another friend's house, sharing her wardrobe and sleeping on the floor. My mom would call from time to time to say hi, ask how I was...but she always assumed everything was fine. Looking back, the lack of care for where your eighth-grade daughter was seems alarming, but for me it was normal. There were no rules. No curfews. This is the age where I started smoking marijuana, drinking and dabbling.

During my high school years, I continued to party. My parents would think nothing of walking past our bedroom where we had three friends with a bottle of vodka, rolling a joint. Their friends began partying openly with us. Bringing us kids into their party amplified the fighting, and the pushing and shoving worsened. I needed to get out so I moved in with my boyfriend's family. When I turned 18, I worked full time, continued high school, and paid for my own apartment. I realized that I did not have to participate in the life that my mom chose.

I worked for the rest of my teenage years and twenties. While my friends worked part-time through college, I was paying rent, a car loan, and working for a Finance & Accounting firm. I pushed myself so hard because I had no one else to count on besides myself. I wanted to prove the statistics wrong and I did. I never attended college because of a desire to create my own life; I believed even without a higher education I would succeed. For 10 years I worked for a Wall Street firm. I made great money and achieved "success," but not the success that made me feel fulfilled, so I left that behind to become what I am today. Today I am at peace. My life is what I have created, without the help of anything or anyone else. Statistically speaking, I should be a victim to my upbringing. I should be barely scraping by, living a life fueled by alcohol as a failure, but I am not. I chose to take what I saw before me as a lesson to do better.

I sit here writing this at 33 years old. I am a married mother of three. I live a fairly normal life with my family. I am a full-time realtor and own an online business. I chose to walk away from my investment career to give my children the time, care and dedication that was taken from me. It is times like this that I look back and say, thank you, life, for kicking me in the dirt over and over again, so I would develop into a strong, independent woman. Thank you, life, for the Ziffers and other families that allowed me to flourish and not be a victim to my upbringing. Thank you, life, for being unfair because a glorious Lotus blooms in the mud.

This has all made me look back at the old days. I now realize how much the kindness, generosity and compassion of the Ziffers truly changed my life. They were the only normal I knew amidst a life of chaos. I am sure that at many times my presence in their home or tagging along on their family trips was a burden for them but they never allowed me to feel that. I have told them as an adult and mother myself, how truly thankful I am to have had them in my life. They chose to step in when my mom chose to check out. They chose to honor my father's wishes where my stepfather would not. They stepped up, without obligation or incentive, to do the right thing. I cannot express how much I honor them as individuals and as a family. I honor what they have done for me, more so as an adult, because I understand my past in a different light now.

I would love the opportunity to pay it forward by adopting an older foster child one day. Being able to take in a 10-12-year-old child, help them to explore their interests, mold them into a productive and driven adult would be such an honor for me and my husband. I hope to do for someone else what the Ziffers and other families did for me.

After meeting with Lynn, I contacted Ann and Greg Ziffer. In my email to Ann, I asked her to share a bit about herself and how she and her husband became such wonderful people. This is her reply: *Greg and I were very close with Lynn's parents. When her dad, Terry, passed away and things started going downhill, our only hope was that we could give Lynn and Garrett some normalcy. That is why our door was always open to them. Yes, there was always enough food if they wanted to eat with us. Yes, there was always somewhere for them to sleep if they wanted to. We were happy to be able to share our lives, and family, with them. I used to have a plaque that read, "It doesn't matter what car you drive, where you live, what clothes you wear or how much money you have in the bank. What matters is the impact you have on the life of a child." We are so happy to have been a safe haven for them and humbled that we were able to have an impact on their lives.*

I am grateful to Lynn and the Ziffers for their willingness to share this story, and I know this story will reach the hearts of many. Each act of kindness, no matter how great or how small, adds more kindness and light into the world.

CHAPTER *Twenty-One*

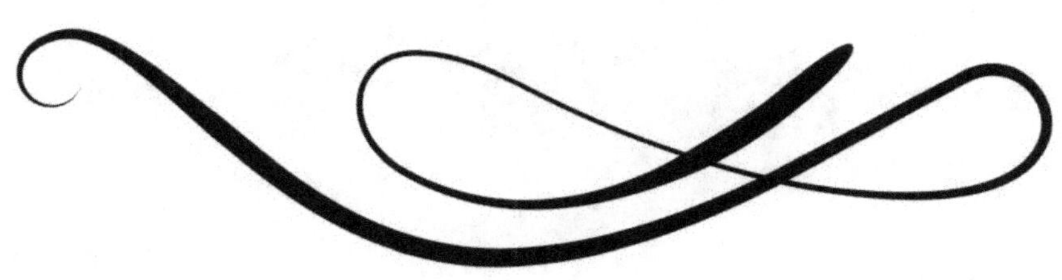

Peace, Prayers & Affirmations

GIULIANA MELO

Giuliana Melo is a certified Angel Intuitive and angel card reader by Doreen Virtue. She is also a certified Mind, Body, Spirit & Reiki Practitioner. She is a bestselling contributing author of 365 DaysOfAngelPrayers and 365 Moments of Grace. She has also written in 4 other multi-author compilations.

Giuliana is an inspirational woman warrior. Giuliana was diagnosed with cancer in 2011. Her journey through cancer reached a low when she pleaded with God, "Why me?" That moment was pivotal in her life in that she heard "Why Not Me?". That answer opened the way for healing, and allowed her to expand her spiritual awareness.

She recently retired from 32 years in Health Care and has an extensive medical background. She is married 29 years and has an 18 year old son.

Connect with Giuliana

Email: jmelo10@shaw.ca

Websites

www.giulianamelo.com

Social Media

www.facebook.com/healwithgiulianamelo

www.twitter.com/Jmelo10Julie

DEDICATION

This chapter is dedicated to Peace of our Lord Jesus Christ in whom all my Power lies.

Peace Prayers &Affirmations

GIULIANA MELO

The definition of peace is:

1. Undisturbed, quiet, tranquil.
2. Freedom from war and violence.

The definition of love is:

1. Feelings, states, attitudes of affection and pleasure.
2. A person or thing that is the object of our love.

I am only one person; however, I possess the peace of God within me. I am love, I come from love and I return to love. "A Course in Miracles" teaches,

"There is no peace but the peace of God." That is what exists inside me. I may not be able to stop a war, but I can create peace within me, my family, my home, my friends, my coworkers and wherever I go. I can control the energy I bring into any space. I truly want to be a reason others believe in the goodness that is God within each of us.

How do we humans co-create peace? By:

1. Loving
2. Offering kindness
3. Giving consideration
4. Sharing gratitude
5. Clearing negativity from our life
6. Meditating
7. Praying

8. Being understanding
9. Practicing compassion
10. Experiencing Joy
11. Staying in the light of God and in the Vibration of the Divine

The path to peace is to find it within each of us and then to spread it out into the world like a ripple on a pond.

Surround yourself with people who emulate love, kindness and peace. Think Peace. Speak Peace. Act Peaceful.

Practice this Recipe for Peace

- Remember to always voice kindness.
- Listen with compassion.
- Be charitable with your hands,
- Use your mind for truth,
- And always love with all your heart and soul!

I hope that the following pages of prayers and affirmations help bring peace into your life.

Peace Prayer #1

Dear God, Universe, Source, Creator,

You have taught me that a peaceful heart is one that acknowledges our oneness. Help me carry only love and peace in my heart. Thank you for your Divine Grace and Favor. You are the Light of that Grace. You are the hope I seek. You are leader of Peace and those of us who are peacemakers.

Amen

Peace Prayer #2

Dear Lord God, Heavenly King, Fountain of Peace,

We come to you today for your Supreme Presence, strength and love during these times of intense energy. We lift all our prayers of peace to you. We ask that you pour down your golden white light to restore peace and harmony to our homes, the earth, and all the creatures who live here. Please help us to see through the eyes of kindness, compassion and love. It is right and good. For this we humbly pray.

Amen

Peace Prayer #3

Dear God,

Today I come to you for help to release all the fears that have only served to hold me back. I ask

You to help me release the past and to see the lessons it gives and the value in those lessons.

I feel your grace and your favor and I embrace it with my whole heart. I recognize the inner power that is indeed You within my heart and my soul. I look forward to my future. I am open to receiving my blessings. I thank you.

Amen.

Peace Prayer #4

Dear Mother Mary and Father God,

I come to you now to humbly ask for the healing power of Peace. I ask for your help for those children of the light that can't seem to let go of ego. I ask for a life of harmony for all of us. I ask for your help in letting go of grievances so that they may be replaced with compassion, understanding, kindness and acceptance.

Please send Archangel Michael and his legions of mercy angels to surround and protect us all. I also ask for Archangels Chamuel and Uriel, angels of peace, to help us all live in union with You and each other.

Thank you and so it is.

Amen.

Peace Prayer #5

The Peace of God is within us. It resides in our hearts and minds. It all depends on your determination to live in peace with each person you encounter. We must make every effort to do what leads to peace. Turn from ego and resolve to do good. Seek peace and pursue it. Be kind and compassionate.

Amen

Peace Prayer of St. Francis

Lord, make me an instrument of your peace.
Where there is hatred, let me sow love;
Where there is injury, pardon;
Where there is doubt, faith;
Where there is despair, hope;
Where there is darkness, light;
Where there is sadness, joy.
O, Divine Master, grant that I may not so much
seek to be consoled as to console;
To be understood as to understand;
To be loved as to love;
For it is in giving that we receive;
It is in pardoning that we are pardoned; and in dying
we are born to eternal life.
~Unknown, ca 1915

Affirmations for Peace

I am open to being an instrument of peace.

I am peace.

I am peaceful.

I speak with kindness.

I am Love.

I am one with Source.

I am perfect, whole, and complete.

I bring positive thoughts wherever I go.

I am Light.

I am created by God and I am filled with love, light and goodness.

I am forgiving.

I can forgive.

I deserve forgiveness.

I let go of my grievances for I know that is how I receive my blessings from the Universe.

I release the past.

I am safe.

I am loving and kind and extend those gifts to others.

I listen with an open heart and an open mind.

I value the opinion of others.

I am harmony.

I create peace within me and take that out into the world.

Peace begins with me.

"Peace does not mean an absence of conflicts; differences will always be there. Peace means solving these differences through peaceful means; through dialogues, education, knowledge; and through human ways."
~Dalai Lama

There is no peace but the peace of God. I release thoughts that don't give me peace of mind. I give my cares to God.

Amen.

ANGELS OF PEACE

To invoke an angel means to call on, ask for help, speak to and communicate with one.

Angels are gifts from God. Messengers. They are supreme light beings. Angels can bring peace to your heart, home and life. Angels bring in harmony. They offer trustworthy guidance. Surrender all cares to God and His angels. They will bring the speedy resolution of any conflict. Angels to call on for peace are:

- Archangel Chamuel—his name means "He who sees God." He is a bringer of love and global Peace. Peace comes when we remember that only love is real. His colour vibration may appear to you as pale pink or pale green. He will also help you locate lost objects when asked.
- Archangel Uriel—his name means "God is light." He is the angel of wisdom and philosophy, and he illuminates our minds with insights and new ideas. He is a bringer of peace. His colour vibration may appear to you as red or yellow.
- Archangel Raguel—his name means "God's friend." He will help us with Peace, Harmony and Divine order. He will bring resolution when we have an argument or a misunderstanding. He will also help us attract new friends. He is an angel of justice. He also helps with forgiveness, bringing healing to ourselves and others, thus restoring peace and harmony. His colour vibration is pale dark blue. Angels resonate on a high frequency and may also come to you in flashes of light.

To invoke these three angels just say: "Dear Angels Chamuel, Uriel, Raguel, I invite you into my life. Please bring peace and calm to my spirit and to that of others' in my life. Thank you.

The first step is asking them to help, then when we allow that help into our life, we believe they are helping us and we can open our arms to minister their help. Angels love when we are grateful. So remember to thank them. Angels truly have brought peace into my life.

With this Divine Team I know I am supported and I know that, no matter what, I will be ok. They love us. There is nothing we could ever do to change that. They will give us with the peace within that fills us up to go out and be PEACE and spread PEACE. I wish you all Peace.

Coloring will help you move out any energy that isn't peaceful. When you are feeling anxious, it may just be pent-up energy that needs to be expressed. Enjoy these coloring sheets lovingly created by Lori Farrell of Twisted Art Designs.

PEACE

PEACE

PEACE
Starts
Within
Your

IN CLOSING...

"Darkness cannot drive out darkness;
only light can do that.
Hate cannot drive out hate;
only love can do that."
~Martin Luther King, Jr.

I hope you've enjoyed the stories and essays that make up this collection. More importantly, I hope you took some time to reflect on what peace means to you. Perhaps you've gained some insight from the previous pages, and hopefully they've left you inspired to take action and do your part to bring peace to our world.

Remember, love is transformative, and peace is an inside job—peace starts with you and me. Can we drown out the darkness? Perhaps not entirely, but each small act of kindness will shine compassion into the world, and over time, collectively, we will outshine the darkness and hate, for we are *The Peacemakers.*

www.ingramcontent.com/pod-product-compliance
Lightning Source LLC
Chambersburg PA
CBHW070439120726
47910CB00003B/848